Oregon
Real Estate Pre-License
Finance

2nd Edition

Oregon Real Estate Pre-license Finance

Executive Editor: Sara Glassmeyer

Project Manager: Arlin Kauffman,
LEAP Publishing Services

Developmental Editor: Molly Armstrong-Paschal

Art and Cover Composition: Chris Dailey

Cover Image: ProSchools

© 2016 OnCourse Learning

ALL RIGHTS RESERVED. No part of this work covered by the copyright herein may be reproduced, transmitted, stored, or used in any form or by any means graphic, electronic, or mechanical, including but not limited to photocopying, recording, scanning, digitizing, taping, web distribution, information networks, or information storage and retrieval systems, except as permitted under Section 107 or 108 of the 1976 United States Copyright Act, without the prior written permission of the publisher.

> For product information and technology assistance, contact us at
> **OnCourse Learning and Sales Support, 1-855-733-7239.**
> For permission to use material from this text or product.

Library of Congress Control Number: 2015951044

ISBN-10: 1629801402
ISBN-13: 978-1-62980-140-7

OnCourse Learning
3100 Cumberland Blvd, Suite 1450
Atlanta, GA 30339
USA

Visit us at **www.oncoursepublishing.com**

Printed in the United States of America
2 3 4 5 6 7 20 19 18 17 16

Finance Laws

Overview

In this lesson we examine the legal aspects of financing in a real estate transaction. Provisions in the note and mortgage used in the financial transaction are explained. The lesson concludes with an overview of laws designed to protect the consumer involved in the mortgage lending process.

Objectives

Upon completion of this lesson, the student should be able to:

1. Define and describe the contents of a promissory note and a mortgage.
2. State the reasons for prepayment penalties.
3. Describe the difference between buying "subject to" and "assuming" a mortgage or deed of trust.
4. Explain the differences between a lien theory state and a title theory state.
5. Explain what happens in a judicial and a nonjudicial foreclosure.
6. Explain and describe an agreement of sale.
7. Describe various loan payment plans.
8. Explain how financial institutions use reserves to insure payment of taxes and insurance.
9. Explain the priorities involved in recording mortgages.
10. Define and describe the following forms of financing:
    a. Fixed- and adjustable-rate mortgages
    b. First and junior mortgages
    c. Wraparound mortgages
    d. Purchase money mortgages
    e. Participation mortgages
    f. Security agreements

       g. Package mortgages
       h. Blanket mortgages
       i. Home equity loans and lines of credit
       j. Open-end and closed-end mortgages
       k. Construction loans
11. Describe the financing legislation that affects mortgage lending, including the Truth In Lending Act and Regulation Z, the Real Estate Settlement Procedures Act (RESPA), the new TILA/RESPA Integrated Disclosure Rule (TRID), the Equal Credit Opportunity Act (ECOA) and the Federal Flood Insurance Program.

Financial Instruments

A person who wants to borrow money may hypothecate (pledge) as security for the loan real property he owns or is to acquire with the funds from the loan. Depending upon the laws of the state, the document used to pledge the real property is called a mortgage or a deed of trust (or trust deed).

----- NOTES -----

In a mortgage transaction there are two instruments given to the lender in return for the loan:
1. A promissory note or bond
2. A mortgage or a deed of trust (trust deed)

In such a transaction, a **promissory note** or bond must always accompany the mortgage. A bond may be used by the government or a private corporation to borrow money. A promissory note is used in residential transactions. A valid promissory note signed by the borrower and given to the lender provides legally acceptable evidence of the borrower's debt and his promise to repay the debt. It establishes:
- who is the borrower.
- who is the lender.
- the amount of the debt.
- the interest rate.
- the terms of repayment.

The mortgage or deed of trust provides security for the loan.

A note may be a negotiable instrument. A **negotiable instrument** is a written, unconditional promise to pay, on demand or at a specified future time, a sum of money "to order" or "to bearer," signed by its maker or payor (the borrower). Other types of negotiable instruments are checks, money orders and drafts. Where there is more than one borrower, all would sign and generally would be "jointly and severally liable" for payment of the note. Each payor would be individually liable to the payee for payment of the entire amount of the note, not just a proportional part.

If the note is negotiable, the payee may transfer the note to another party, by writing his name across the back of the note. This signature is called an **endorsement**. When notes used in real estate loan transactions are sold, the endorser may endorse it "without recourse," making it a qualified endorsement. Under a qualified endorsement, the endorser has no liability for default on the note. The holder of the note would have recourse only against the maker of the note and the property securing the note.

A note may be sold for the amount owed, less than the amount owed (at a discount) or more than the amount owed (at a premium). In each case, the note holder is entitled to receive from the maker of the note all of the payments specified in the note regardless of the amount paid for the note.

> **For Example**
>
> An investor who purchases a note with a balance of $50,000 for $30,000 has a right to sue for the $50,000 owed or foreclose on the property to get $50,000, not just the $30,000 paid for the note.

Provisions

A note contains a number of provisions relating to repayment of the debt.

As it is an installment note, it will specify the amount of the payments to be made and when, where and to whom they are to be made.

It may contain a **prepayment privilege**, or right to prepay. This gives the borrower the right to pay all or some of the outstanding principal balance during the term of the note before it is due, either with or without a prepayment charge. A prepayment privilege could be written simply as an "or more" clause, allowing the borrower to pay the specified amount or more without a penalty.

A prepayment privilege could include a **prepayment penalty** clause providing for a fee for the privilege of paying off the loan ahead of schedule. The fee may be a percentage of the original principal balance or an amount of interest that would accrue over a specified period of time, e.g., six months of interest. Generally, when funds are plentiful and demand for loans is low, a lender would charge the prepayment penalty provided for in the note. If there were a tight money market (meaning funds are in short supply) and demand for loans was high, despite higher interest rates, the lender might waive the prepayment penalty in order to encourage borrowers to pay off their loans early.

A note may contain a **lock-in clause** prohibiting any loan prepayment, at least for a certain period.

It may include a **late payment penalty** provision to create motivation for timely payment. The penalty could be a specified dollar figure or a percentage of the overdue payment.

An **acceleration clause** allows the lender to declare the entire unpaid loan balance due upon a default of any of the terms or conditions of the document, including failure to pay insurance premiums, property taxes, or the principal and interest on the debt.

Most nongovernment real estate notes have an **alienation clause** (or due-on-sale clause or call provision). It provides that, if title is alienated (transferred to another) without the lender's prior written consent, the lender may, at its option, call the loan due at once and require immediate payment in full of all sums owed. This provision prohibits assumption of the loan without the lender's permission, so the lender can require that the new borrower submit to qualification on the same basis as the original borrower to ensure that his risk is not increased.

Title Subject To vs. Assumption

When a borrower sells his property, unless the alienation clause requires that the loan be paid in full, the purchaser may take title to the property with the lien remaining against the property. In doing so, he may either assume responsibility for payment or not assume such responsibility:

- If the buyer were not to be responsible for making the payments to the lender, he would take **title subject to** the existing loan.
- If he is to be responsible for making payments to the lender he would **assume and agree to pay** the loan.

> **For Example**
> Basil is willing to sell Rosemary a property for $200,000. There is an existing loan outstanding, which by the time the sale closes will have a balance of $150,000. Basil agrees to take a $30,000 down payment and a purchase money mortgage and note for $170,000. Rosemary will make payments to Basil on the $170,000 note out of which payments Basil will continue to pay on the existing $150,000 debt. In this case, Rosemary is taking title that is subject to a loan and is not responsible for the payments on that loan.

When the deed to a property contains a clause stating that the grantee (buyer) takes title subject to the existing loan, this shows that the grantee is aware that the property is encumbered by that loan but assumes no personal liability for the debt. The seller retains all personal liability for the debt in case of default, foreclosure sale and a deficiency. If a foreclosure sale brings less than the amount owed on the loan, the lender can take action for a deficiency judgment against the original borrower but not against the grantee. Unfortunately, the grantee would lose the property and his equity.

If the seller does not pay off the existing loan upon sale but does not wish to be primarily responsible for the existing loan after the sale, he would have the buyer assume and agree to pay the loan, if the lending institution permits it. A buyer who assumes and agrees to pay an existing mortgage is assuming primary responsibility for the payments and agreeing to make the payments as per the terms of the note directly to the lender.

However, the seller still has secondary liability for the loan. This means:
- if the buyer were to default and the lender were to sue on the note, or if there were a foreclosure sale and a deficiency, the buyer would be subject to a judgment.
- if the buyer could not satisfy the judgment, the lender could sue the seller for payment, even if the lender had approved the buyer and collected an assumption fee.

While a lender may allow a loan to be assumed, assumptions are quite rare today. It is better for the seller to have the purchaser qualify for his own loan than to remain responsible in case of default by the purchaser.

In order for the seller to be relieved of all liability for payment of an assumed mortgage, the seller must obtain from the lender a substitution of borrower or release of liability agreement. This would result in novation of the contract, with the buyer totally replacing the seller as a party to the contract. A lender would agree to a novation only if the buyer could satisfy the lender's credit and financial standards for loan qualification.

To review, consider these situations:
- When the buyer takes title subject to the existing loan, the seller has all the liability and the buyer has none.
- When the buyer assumes and agrees to pay an existing loan, the buyer has primary liability and the seller has secondary liability.
- When the buyer assumes and agrees to pay the assumed loan and the seller obtains a release of liability from the lender, the buyer has all the liability and the seller has none.

Title Subject To vs. Assumption

Title Subject to Existing Loan

Buyer — 170K → Seller — 150K → Lender

Assumption

Buyer — 20K → Seller

Buyer — 150K → Lender

When a buyer takes title subject to an existing loan, or assumes an existing loan, he should request a reduction certificate, or beneficiary statement from the lender. This will show the exact status of the loan at closing, including the balance due and interest rate. This is the same information shown on an estoppel certificate (certificate of no defense) that a borrower may sign when his loan is sold.

----- MORTGAGE -----

With a note, the lender has the borrower's promise to pay the debt but nothing to secure that promise. A **mortgage** is a written contract pledging real property the borrower owns or will own to secure the debt.

Depending on the state, a mortgage can convey title to the lender or simply create a lien for the lender:
- Most states operate under the lien theory of mortgages. This means a mortgage creates a specific voluntary lien against the borrower's property, that may be enforced by foreclosure, where the borrower's rights to the property are terminated.
- In title theory states, the mortgage conveys title to the lender, and title is returned to the borrower when the loan is repaid.
- In intermediate theory states, the mortgage gives the lender a lien but allows him to take title without foreclosure if the borrower defaults.

Finance Laws

Provisions

A mortgage may contain a number of provisions that are not included in the note. These clauses are not, however, required in order for the mortgage to be legally enforceable.

- The borrower may be required to pay all taxes, assessments, liens or encumbrances that could have priority over the mortgage.
- An insurance clause may require the borrower to keep the property insured against fire loss for at least the amount of the loan balance until the debt is fully paid. The insurance company must be acceptable to the lender and must name the lender as co-payee.
- The borrower may be required to maintain the property in good condition at all times, making all necessary repairs promptly to assure that the value of the property is being maintained.
- A **defeasance clause** states that, if the loan is paid according to the terms of the note and the other covenants are fulfilled, the lender will release the lien, so the borrower will regain clear title.
- If the property is rental property, an **assignment of rents clause** provides that the rents from the property are assigned to the lender as security for payment of the debt. As long as the borrower does not default in the loan terms, he may collect and retain the rents. If he defaults and the note is accelerated, or if he abandons the property, the lender has the right to enter the property, take possession and manage it, and collect all rents earned by the property.
- A **request for notice of default** clause provides for notification to the lender if another lien against the property is in default so the lender may take action to prevent loss due to foreclosure of the other lien.

Mortgagor and Mortgagee

In return for a mortgage loan, the borrower gives the lender a note promising to repay the loan and a mortgage securing the promise.

- Because the borrower gives the mortgage, the borrower is called the **mortgagor**.
- Because the lender is receiving the mortgage, the lender is called the **mortgagee**.

Through the mortgage, the mortgagor gives a lien to the mortgagee, which the mortgagee holds during the period of the indebtedness. However, the mortgagor (borrower) holds the title to the real property and retains legal ownership of the property even while the property is encumbered by the lien.

When a mortgage is paid off and the mortgagor requests it, the mortgagee must acknowledge **satisfaction** of the mortgage. This is recorded in order to clear the mortgage lien from the records.

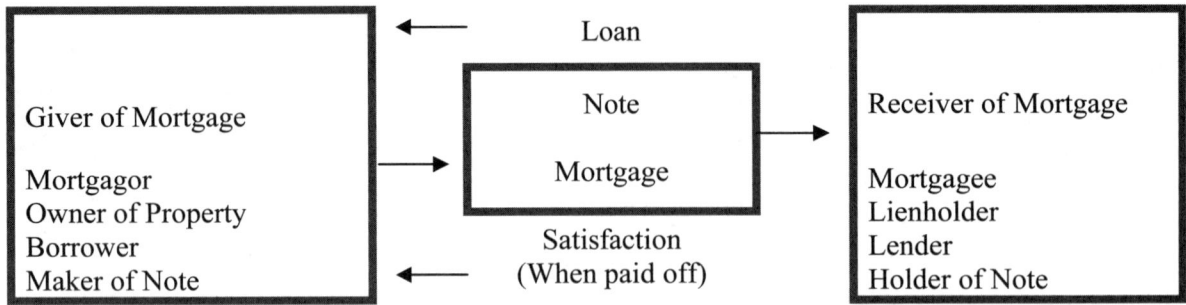

If a mortgagor defaults on the promises he makes in the note or mortgage, the mortgagee may, depending on state law, have the right to:
- sue on the note to obtain a judgment lien against the borrower.
- file for a **judicial foreclosure and sale**. This would result in the property being foreclosed and sold through court action.
- file for **strict foreclosure**. This would result in judicial foreclosure and the property given to the lender instead of being sold. In most states this is not allowed.
- have the property foreclosed through a nonjudicial foreclosure, if the mortgage contains a **power of sale clause**. This clause gives the lender the power to sell the property without a judicial foreclosure, upon default. The actual sale could be executed by the lender or its representative, typically referred to as a trustee.

A foreclosure wipes out the borrower's **equitable right of redemption** (or equity of redemption). This is the right to pay off the mortgage debt plus interest and costs prior to the foreclosure.

A **foreclosure sale** is an auction sale to the highest bidder.
- If the sale produces an amount in excess of the amount needed to pay off the foreclosure costs and unpaid debt, the excess is given to the foreclosed mortgagor.
- If not enough is bid to cover the foreclosure costs and the amount of the unpaid debt, the lender cannot cancel the sale but may obtain a **deficiency judgment** against the mortgagor for the difference, unless state statute prohibits such a judgment or the loan is a **nonrecourse loan** (one in which the lender has no recourse against the borrower personally).

In many states there is a **statutory right of redemption** after the sale, allowing the mortgagor a period of time after the foreclosure sale, to buy back the property.

----- DEED OF TRUST -----

A **deed of trust** (also called a **trust deed**) is a form of mortgage that is available in many states, particularly those that do not have laws allowing for a power of sale provision in a mortgage. It has the same type of provisions as a mortgage with the major difference being in provisions relating to foreclosure.

With a deed of trust, the borrower is called a **trustor** or **grantor**. As does a mortgage, in a lien theory state, the deed of trust gives the lender a lien, not title. Therefore, the trustor holds the title to the property. The lender is called a **beneficiary**. The trustor makes his loan payments to the beneficiary.

In the deed of trust, the trustor gives a third party (called the **trustee**) a power of sale, allowing the trustee to sell the property without court approval. If the grantor defaults, the beneficiary can sue on the note, file for judicial foreclosure, or instruct the trustee to conduct a trustee's sale. After a trustee's sale (or after a statutory redemption period, if the state law provides for one), the trustee will convey title to the high bidder, through a trustee's deed.

If the grantor pays off the loan, the beneficiary will instruct the trustee to issue a deed of reconveyance. This is recorded to show the lien has been satisfied. It serves the same purpose as a satisfaction of mortgage does for a mortgage.

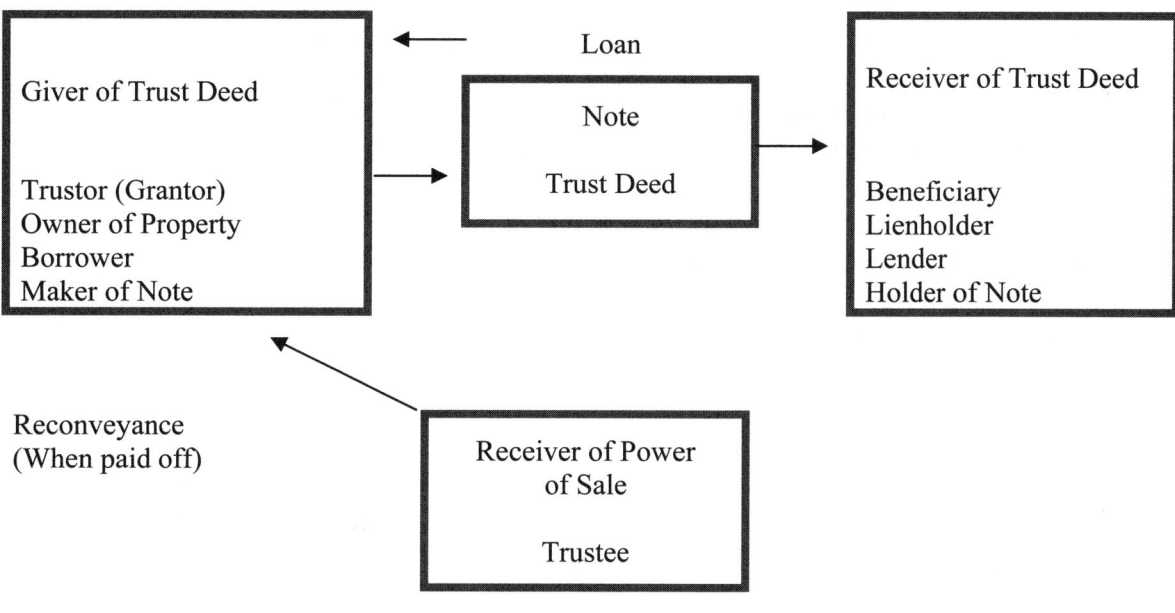

----- SELLER FINANCING -----

It is not necessary for a person to obtain a loan from a third party lender in order to purchase real estate. In some instances, the seller is willing and able to finance the purchase of his property for the new buyer. The buyer pays a certain amount of money as a down payment and then makes periodic payments to the seller on the balance of the selling price over an agreed period of time.

Purchase Money Mortgage
The financing arrangement may be handled by the buyer giving the seller a note for the balance of the purchase price plus a mortgage securing the note. Simultaneously, at closing, the seller gives the buyer a deed to the property. The buyer holds title to the property and the seller has a lien against the buyer's property, as a mortgagee. When the seller takes back a mortgage as full or partial payment for the property, the mortgage is

d a **purchase money mortgage**. When a deed to the buyer is recorded at the same as a purchase money mortgage, the purchase money mortgage will have priority any liens the buyer may place against the property.

Contract for Deed (Land Sales Contract)

As an alternative to a purchase money mortgage, the seller could provide the same terms of credit to the buyer under a contract that provides for the buyer to receive a deed to the property only after the buyer has paid the full balance of the purchase price. This type of contract may be referred to by such names as **contract for deed**, **agreement of sale**, **land sales contract**, land contract, real estate contract, installment sale contract, real property sales contract, or conditional contract of sale. Generally, the use of such a contract is popular when there is little money available through conventional means, when the buyer cannot qualify for a conventional loan at reasonable rates or cannot afford a normal down payment and closing costs.

Under the terms of the contract for deed, the purchaser pays for the property in installments while the seller retains title until the property is paid for in full. This makes it the least secure method of financing for the buyer, as the buyer does not have title and does not have absolute assurance of receiving title upon performance of the contract. To protect himself, the buyer should see that:
- the contract is recorded. If not recorded, it would be valid between the parties but not against those with no knowledge of it.
- a collection escrow is set up, with the parties sharing the cost of maintaining the escrow. A deed would be placed in escrow at the time the agreement is made, an escrow agent would collect the payments for the seller, and upon fulfillment of the terms of the contract, the escrow agent would deliver the deed in satisfaction to the buyer.

Under this contract, the seller is called the **vendor**. As title remains in his name, the vendor is said to have the legal title to the property.

The buyer is called the **vendee**. He has a legal interest in the property (called **equitable title**) that entitles him to a conveyance of the legal title when all contract payments have been made. In most instances the contract provides for the vendee to get possession of the property and pay property taxes, property insurance premiums and all maintenance expenses of the property for the duration of the contract, while he pays for the property in regular installments.

The vendor, however, remains primarily liable for the payment of insurance premiums, taxes, and any underlying mortgage payments.

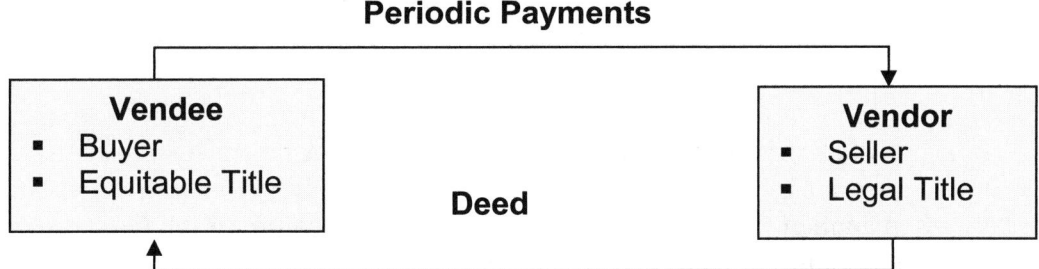

The contract encumbers the vendor's title and is a cloud on the title until he delivers a deed to the vendee, receives a quitclaim deed from the vendee releasing the vendee's interest, or takes legal action to remove the vendee's interest from the title.

If the vendee defaults on the contract, the vendor may, depending on state law, be able to:
- sue for any delinquent payment.
- accelerate the balance due and sue for payment of the balance.
- sue for strict foreclosure.
- sue for specific performance.
- forfeit the buyer's interest, if the contract contains a forfeiture clause.

Loan Types

----- TYPES OF MORTGAGES -----

Names are often applied to mortgages to describe a certain feature of the loan, such as its purpose, the type of interest charged, the payment method, etc. The mortgage itself would not show the name, but a feature of that document would cause people to use the name to describe it. In most instances, one document may be described using a number of terms. This will become clearer as we go on.

Interest Rates
Fixed
A **fixed-rate mortgage** provides for an interest rate that will remain fixed for the entire term of the loan.

Variable
A mortgage that provides for the interest rate to go up or down according to some indicator, (e.g., an index tied to Treasury bill rates), may be called an **adjustable-rate mortgage (ARM)**, **variable-rate mortgage**, **flexible-rate mortgage**, **renegotiated-rate mortgage** or **rollover mortgage**. It has a variable interest rate provision that allows the interest rate to be increased in an inflationary economy or decreased when market conditions cause current interest rates to drop. Generally, the loans have a low introductory rate for a limited time. After that, the interest rate will be adjusted to eventually equal the index rate plus a margin rate added to cover the lender's expenses and profit.

Adjustable- or variable-rate mortgages allow for changes in interest rates on a fairly regular basis, usually every six months or every year. So that these loans do not become instantly unaffordable when rates rise, there may be interest caps, limiting the rate increase at any one time and/or over the loan term, and payment caps, limiting the amount the monthly payment may increase. A payment cap may cause **negative amortization** when the capped payment does not cover all of the interest being charged on the loan and the unpaid interest is added to the loan balance. Renegotiated rate or rollover mortgages provide for a fixed interest rate initially (e.g., the first three, four or five years), followed by a new interest rate, renegotiated to reflect current market conditions, that will remain fixed until the time for the next renegotiation.

Payment Methods
Term (Straight)
A **term** (or **straight** or **interest-only**) **mortgage** provides for payment of interest only, with no amortization (reduction of the loan balance) during the term of the loan. The word "term" describes the fact that the entire principal amount is due at the end of the term. The word "straight" describes the fact that the loan amount, as well as the interest

Finance Laws

payment, is straight, or level, throughout the term. The payment made at the end of the term would be called a **balloon payment**, as it would be considerably larger than the previous payments.

Reverse Annuity

A **reverse mortgage** or **reverse annuity mortgage** is a loan secured by real estate that is due on default or when the property is sold or no longer used as a principal residence. It is designed to enable a person who already owns real estate to convert some of his equity into cash. It is available to persons age 62 or older who own their home and need cash to meet their expenses.

This mortgage provides for the lender to pay the borrower funds in a lump sum or in monthly advances and/or through a line of credit. It is a negative amortization loan with compound interest. Each month interest is added to the principal loan balance, causing the total amount owed to increase significantly as interest is compounded (charged on the additional interest).

Another option is that the lender gains a share of equity with each dollar advanced.

Amortized

An **amortized loan** involves gradual liquidation or extinction of the loan during the term of the loan through periodic payments to principal as well as interest. The term "amortization" can also be used in connection with paying off a land sales contract or with writing off depreciation for tax purposes.

A **partially amortized (balloon)** mortgage provides for some, but not total, amortization during the term of the mortgage. The term "balloon" refers to the large payment needed to pay off the unamortized principal balance during or at the end of the loan period.

A **fully amortized (self-liquidating)** mortgage provides for periodic payments resulting in the loan being repaid in its entirety by the end of the mortgage term without the need for a balloon payment. Methods of payment used for these loans might be level payment, a graduated payment mortgage, budget mortgage, and direct principal reduction.

The **level payment** mortgage provides for equal payments of principal and interest throughout the loan period. As the principal balance is paid down, the portion of each payment that applies to principal increases while the portion applying to interest decreases. However, the total payment remains the same.

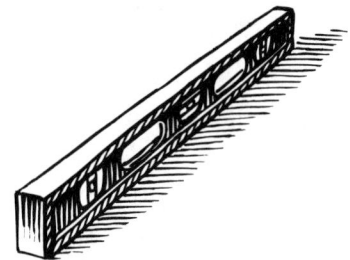

A **graduated payment** mortgage provides for payments to start out relatively low, rise at a set rate over a set period, e.g., five years, and then remain constant for the duration of the loan. During the initial years of the loan, mortgage payments would be lower than the amount required to pay the interest due and amortize the loan by the end of the loan term. This results in initial negative amortization. The difference needed to get back on schedule to pay off the loan by the maturity date is made up by higher loan payments in the future.

Finance Laws

A **budget mortgage** or PITI mortgage (for principal, interest, taxes and insurance), provides that an amount equal to 1/12 of the estimated annual property insurance premiums, property taxes, homeowners' association dues and/or special assessments, if any, will be paid to the mortgagee, together with the monthly installment of principal and interest. The lender holds the amount paid for these items in a reserve account (also called an escrow account or an impound account) until they are due to be paid. Because this plan reduces the incidence of default and foreclosure, it is required for FHA and VA loans. For other loans, lenders may impose the requirement themselves.

With a **direct principal reduction** loan, periodic payments include a fixed amount of principal, for example, $1,000 per month, plus interest on the unpaid balance. Under this payment method, the periodic payments get smaller with each payment as less interest is added on each month.

Loan Priority
First and Second Mortgages
In the absence of fraud or actual knowledge of a prior lien, a mortgage recorded first has priority over any mortgage recorded later, regardless of the dates the two mortgages were executed. The priority of a mortgage, like the priority of a deed, is established by the date it was recorded, not by the date it was executed.

However this priority may be changed with a **subordination clause**. Subordination is an agreement to waive some rights in favor of another. The word "subordination" means to place in a lower position. So, a subordination clause puts a loan in an inferior priority by allowing another lien to take precedence.

> *For Example:* Guy and Barb Dwyer purchased a piece of vacant property for $200,000. They put $50,000 down, and the seller carried back a mortgage for $150,000 for a term of 10 years. They plan to build on the property in five years, prior to paying off the existing mortgage. Without a subordination clause in their mortgage, they will have problems when they try to get financing to build their home. With a subordination clause in the first mortgage giving a new construction loan first priority, they can get their loan.

If the clause is not already in an existing first mortgage, it can be added later by a subordination agreement signed by the first mortgagee.

A subordination clause may be used in first mortgages or trust deeds to make them junior, or it may be used in junior mortgages or trust deeds to keep them junior in the event a first lien is refinanced. It may also be used with the same effect in a real estate contract (contract for deed).

First Mortgage
A mortgage is called a **first mortgage** if there are no other mortgages on the property with prior lien rights.

Junior Mortgage

A **junior mortgage** is a lien on real property that is subordinate to another mortgage that was previously recorded. It may be in second, third, or lower priority. A second mortgage exists when there is one other mortgage that has a prior lien on the property ahead of it; a third mortgage exists when there are two other mortgages that have a prior lien on the property. A purchase money mortgage can sometimes be used as a junior financing instrument if the alienation clause does not require the existing loan to be paid off. Junior liens are somewhat risky. In the event of a foreclosure, mortgages are paid off in the order of their priority. If foreclosure of a prior mortgage does not yield enough to pay liens lower in priority, those liens are wiped out, unpaid. This is one reason why a lender may refuse to accept an estoppel deed (deed in lieu of foreclosure). A **deed in lieu of foreclosure** is a voluntary act of a borrower who is in default to transfer title to the lender by deed. This option may reduce damage to the borrower's credit standing and would save the lender time and money by avoiding foreclosure. The problem for the lender is that the deed would convey title subject to all existing encumbrances, including junior liens that would have been eliminated by a foreclosure.

Wraparound Mortgage

One type of junior mortgage is a wraparound (or wrap). The wrap-around technique may be used in wraparound (or all-inclusive) mortgages or contracts for deed.

A **wraparound mortgage** is a second mortgage, which is subordinate to an existing first and unsatisfied lien on the property. It differs from other junior liens in that the face amount of the wrap includes the amount borrowed on the junior lien plus the amount owed on the first lien. For example, if a person owes $100,000 on a first lien and wants to borrow $10,000, the wraparound second lien would show a face amount of $110,000, not just $10,000. In addition, the wrap has a special agreement between the borrower and junior lender providing that the junior lender will make the payments on the first lien as they become due, out of the total payments made by the borrower.

Loans Classified by Security

Mortgages are also classified based on the type of property used as security for the loan.

Chattel Mortgage and Security Agreement

A **chattel mortgage** is a mortgage lien encumbering only personal property (i.e., chattel). The chattel mortgage has been replaced in many areas of the country by a security agreement regulated by the Uniform Commercial Code.

A **security agreement** between the debtor (borrower) and the secured party (seller or lender) must be in writing unless the secured party is holding the collateral. It describes the rights and obligations of the parties, the property pledged as collateral, and if the collateral relates to fixtures, the real estate. It ensures that, if the debtor fails to pay the debt, the secured party will become the owner of the property pledged as collateral or will have the right to have the property sold to pay the debt.

Package Mortgage

A **package mortgage** is a mortgage using both real property and personal property as security for the loan. Items such as ranges, ovens, refrigerators, freezers, rugs or dishwashers may be included in the sale price of the property but are not considered real property. The purchaser may have a choice of paying cash for these items, financing them separately with a consumer loan, or having them included as security for the mortgage loan. If the mortgage includes such items, it would be referred to as a package mortgage.

This type of loan is used frequently in financing commercial rental properties, such as apartment buildings and office buildings. It enables the borrower to:
- deal with only one lender.
- make his payments uniform throughout the term of the loan.
- distribute his payments over a longer period.

Blanket Mortgage

A **blanket mortgage** is one mortgage that covers more than one parcel of real estate as security.

> **For Example**
> When an owner of six parcels of real property offers all six parcels as security for a mortgage loan, the mortgage is a blanket mortgage.

A borrower with a blanket encumbrance on a subdivision would need a **release clause** (or partial release clause, parcel release clause, or lot release clause) to allow portions of the property to be released from the mortgage lien before the entire loan is repaid. As a certain amount of the debt is paid off, individual parcels may be released if the blanket mortgage has a release clause, relinquishing the lien on individual lots as they are sold.

To ensure that adequate security remains as the parcels are released, a release schedule will require that a greater percentage of the loan be repaid than the parcels represent. For example, it may require payment of 20% of the loan before releasing 10% of the total number of parcels.

In order for the borrower to sell a released parcel with clear title, he needs to record a **partial satisfaction** of mortgage or **partial reconveyance** deed, showing that the parcel has been released from the encumbrance.

Participation Mortgage

A **participation mortgage** is used most often in loans for development of large commercial real estate projects. The lender conditions the loan commitment upon receiving part ownership interest in the development. He earns interest as well as a percentage of the project's net income or its ownership in return for granting the loan or for granting concessions, such as a higher loan-to-value ratio or a lower interest rate.

> **For Example**
>
> When a lender agrees to reduce the interest rate on a loan by ½% in return for a 2% interest in a large commercial complex, this is a participation mortgage.

One version of this is a **shared appreciation (shared equity) mortgage**. In return for a relatively low interest rate, the borrower agrees to share with the lender a sizeable percent (e.g., 30% to 50%) of the appreciation in the value of the property, either after a specified number of years or when title is transferred.

Closed- and Open-End Mortgages

Closed-End Mortgages

Most mortgages are **closed end**. In other words, there is a fixed amount borrowed, and no additional funds can be borrowed without a new note and mortgage.

Open-End Mortgages

An **open-end mortgage** (or mortgage for future advances) allows the borrower to borrow additional funds up to a specified maximum amount without negotiating a new mortgage. (This is similar to using a credit card, with a mortgage making the real property security for repayment.) The lender will authorize a maximum amount that may be borrowed. The borrower may initially borrow less and later borrow the rest, or the borrower may initially borrow the entire amount and then, as he repays the loan, reborrow amounts he has paid off, up to the original loan amount. The note may provide for the interest rate for any new money to be at the original interest rate, or at the market rate at the time the new money is loaned, or for the interest rate for the entire loan to be based on current market rates.

Construction Mortgage

One type of open-end mortgage is a **construction mortgage**. Construction financing is usually designed as a high-interest, short-term loan to finance the cost of labor and materials used during the construction of a new building. It is a form of interim (or temporary) financing, extending from the commencement of the work until the work is completed and the loan is replaced by a more permanent form of financing.

Usually, the lender will not give the full amount of the loan to the borrower up front but will advance funds to the borrower in installments after each inspection of progress on the job. These advances are called **obligatory advances** or draws. The lender may also require the builder to obtain a sufficient performance bond, guaranteeing that the lender will be indemnified if the contractor fails to complete the job.

Finance Laws

Lenders may:
- advance funds at regular intervals, such as monthly, based on the work completed that month.
- pay all bills directly, upon receipt from the borrower.
- disburse funds as stages of work are completed, with final payment withheld until all labor and materials have been paid for (evidenced by lien waivers from the contractors and subcontractors) or until the lien period has expired, to ensure no liens are filed against the property for unpaid work/materials.

Interest is charged on the money only as it is disbursed. The entire loan amount, plus any accumulated interest, is due in full within a short period of time after completion of the project. This allows the builder time to sell the property or refinance the loan with a take-out loan. A **take-out loan** is a long-term loan taken out after construction is completed and used to pay off the construction loan. Often an interim lender will require a commitment by the permanent lender to agree to provide the take-out financing upon completion of construction before it will provide the interim financing.

A construction loan is usually a first mortgage on the property on which improvements are being constructed. Therefore, the land must be free of liens or any existing liens must be subordinated to the construction mortgage before the loan will be granted.

LOAN SECURITY	
Type	**Secured with**
Chattel Mortgage/Security Agreement	Personal Property
Package	Real and Personal Property
Blanket with Release	Multiple Real Property
Interim vs. Take out	Short-term Construction vs. Permanent

----- HOME EQUITY LOANS AND CREDIT LINES ------

A **home equity loan** is most often a junior loan in which the homeowner uses the equity in his home as a basis for a loan. A home equity loan can be used for anything: home improvements, consolidating and paying credit card and consumer debts, car purchases, education, medical expenses, etc.

The main advantage of a home equity loan or line of credit is that the interest paid on a loan of up to $100,000 is tax deductible, regardless of the purpose of the loan.

A **home equity line of credit (HELOC)** is a form of revolving credit in which a person's home serves as collateral. By using his equity in the home, a borrower may qualify for a sizable amount of credit at an interest rate that is relatively low. The borrower is approved for a specific credit limit based on a percentage (e.g., 75 %) of the appraised value of the home less the balance owed on the existing mortgage.

> *For example:*
>
> | | |
> |---:|---:|
> | Appraised Value | $100,000 |
> | Percentage | X 75% |
> | Percentage of Appraised Value | $ 75,000 |
> | Less Mortgage Debt | - $ 40,000 |
> | Potential Credit Line | $ 35,000 |

Once approved, the borrower may utilize funds up to his credit limit whenever he wants. He can access the funds using special checks, a credit card or other means, within restrictions set for use of the credit. Such restrictions might include a minimum amount that must be borrowed each time he draws on the line of credit, a minimum amount that must be outstanding, or an initial advance that must be taken when the line is set up. Typically, interest rates for these credit lines are variable rather than fixed.

Lending Laws

In order to protect consumers in their financial transactions, Congress has passed a number of laws affecting real estate financing:
1) Truth in Lending Act
2) Real Estate Settlement Procedures Act
3) Equal Credit Opportunity Act
4) Flood Disaster Protection Act

Truth in Lending Act (TILA)
Truth in lending regulations are contained in the **Consumer Credit Protection Act** (the **Truth in Lending Act**) and **Regulation Z** issued by the Federal Reserve Board. The law and Regulation Z are administered by the Federal Reserve Board but enforced by various federal agencies. With regard to mortgage bankers, mortgage brokers and real estate brokers, the enforcing agency is the Federal Trade Commission (FTC).

The purpose of the law is to ensure that applicants for consumer credit are given sufficient information about the cost and conditions of the credit or an installment purchase so they can easily compare credit terms offered by various creditors. The Truth in Lending Act only deals with disclosure. It does not set limits on the amount the lenders may charge for credit. Limits on amounts that may be charged are generally imposed through state usury laws.

Application of Truth in Lending
The Truth in Lending Act only applies to consumer loans; that is, loans for personal, family and household purposes. It does not apply to credit extended primarily for business, commercial, or agricultural purposes. Consumer loans are loans payable in four or more installments from creditors (those who extend credit more than 25 times in a year, or five times on loans secured by dwellings). They include loans:
- to acquire owner-occupied real estate containing one or two units.
- to improve or maintain owner-occupied real estate containing one to four units.
- of up to $25,000 secured by personal property.

There are three principal areas covered by the law:
1) Disclosure
2) Rescission
3) Advertising

Disclosures
The creditor must make a number of disclosures to a credit applicant within three business days after receiving a written application for credit. The most prominent of these are the:
- amount financed.
- finance charge.
- annual percentage rate.
- total payments.

The amount financed is the amount of credit provided the borrower (the loan amount).

Finance Laws

The **finance charge** is the dollar amount the credit will cost the borrower over the term of the loan. It includes:
- all money the lender will receive and keep (e.g., interest, loan origination fees, loan finder's fee, assumption fees, discount points paid by the borrower, loan service charges).
- costs incurred by choosing a particular lender that might not be incurred with another lender (such as premiums for credit life insurance or mortgage insurance and fees for inspections required by the lender).

The finance charge does not include:
- closing costs, such as fees for title insurance, recording, property survey, and preparation of deeds, mortgages and other documents to close.
- notary, appraisal, escrow, legal and credit report services.
- other amounts paid into escrow which do not go to the creditor (property taxes and property insurance premiums).

The **annual percentage rate (APR)** is the effective interest rate, reflecting the cost of the credit expressed to the nearest 1/8 of 1% as a yearly rate. It includes finance charges as well as the interest, so it is usually higher than the nominal (stated) interest rate.

The **total of payments** is the dollar amount the borrower will have paid when he has made all of the scheduled payments.

Among other disclosures provided on the lender's disclosure statement are:
- the length of the loan term.
- the amount of the monthly payment.
- any prepayment penalty.
- the amount charged for late payments.

Rescission
For some consumer loans, a borrower has a right to rescind the transaction within three business days of signing the loan documents. Rescission rights apply to a home equity loan, line of credit, or home improvement loan secured by the borrower's principal residence. These rights do not apply to loans to buy or build a principal residence or to consolidate or refinance a loan already secured by the residence with the same creditor without borrowing additional funds.

Advertising
The Truth in Lending Act and Regulation Z regulate advertising of consumer credit, including flyers, billboards, window displays, direct mail literature, telephone solicitation, etc. These regulations apply regardless of who the advertiser is, including real estate brokers and homeowners advertising assumptions of their loans.

The law allows advertisements to show general terms ("low down payment," "reasonable monthly terms," "FHA financing available," or "low interest rates") or to show the annual percentage rate without showing any other credit terms. However, when any specific credit

terms (called **trigger terms**) are used in an ad, they must be credit terms usually accepted by the lender, and the ad must provide other details of the loan, including:
- the loan amount.
- the annual percentage rate.
- the amount or percentage of down payment.
- the number, amount and frequency of payments.
- the fact that the rate may be increased, if that is so.

Trigger terms include the:
- amount or percentage of down payment ("5% down," "95% financing," "$6,200 down").
- amount of any installment payment ("payments 1% per month," "payment less than $1,400 per month").
- number of payments ("360 monthly payments").
- period of repayment ("30 year loan").
- dollar amount of any finance charge ("total financing costs less than $3,000").

Real Estate Settlement Procedures Act (RESPA)

The **Real Estate Settlement Procedures Act (RESPA)** is administered by HUD. It requires lenders to provide borrowers with information about the process of settlement (or closing) of the transaction, so they may make informed decisions regarding the selection of settlement services. The law applies to transactions involving federally related loans to finance a purchase, refinance, or obtain a home equity loan or line of credit using residential real property as security. A federally related residential mortgage

loan is a first or junior loan secured by residential (one- to four-family) real property from a lender who makes over $1,000,000 in residential real estate loans per year.

In an effort to make it easier for consumers to compare key information within loan documentation such as interest rates, closing costs of a loan, monthly payments and loan programs from competing lenders, the Consumer Financial Protection Bureau will be consolidating four separate disclosures into two combined disclosures. This new rule, referred to as TRID (the TILA/RESPA Integrated Disclosure Rule) will be implemented and effective as of October 3, 2015. The first consolidation of forms is that the Good Faith Estimate and the preliminary Truth in Lending Disclosure will be combined into a preliminary disclosure referred to as the Loan Estimate. The Loan Estimate must be given to the buyer no later than three business days after submission of the loan application to the lender. The second form consolidation is that the HUD-1 Form and the final Truth in Lending Disclosure will be merged into a disclosure form known as the Closing Disclosure. The Closing Disclosure will be given to the borrower three business days before the loan is consummated.

The TRID rule has an exemption for those lenders who make five or fewer loans per year. The transactions that are exempted from the requirements set forth in this new rule are Home Equity Lines of Credit, reverse mortgages, cash transactions, commercial purpose loans, mobile home loans and no-interest second mortgages that are made for down payment assistance, and energy efficiency or foreclosure avoidance loans.

Equal Credit Opportunity Act

The **Equal Credit Opportunity Act (ECOA)** prohibits creditors from discriminating against a loan applicant on the basis of:
- race, religion, color, national origin, sex, marital status, or age.
- receipt of income from public assistance programs.
- good faith exercise of rights under the Consumer Credit Protection Act.

As a result, creditors may not:
- on the basis of race, religion, national origin, sex, marital status, or age, make statements discouraging applicants or refuse to grant an account to a creditworthy applicant.
- use sex or marital status in credit-scoring systems.
- ask the marital status of an applicant applying for an unsecured separate account, except in a community property state or as required to comply with state laws.
- inquire into child-bearing intentions or capability or birth control practices, or assume from an applicant's age that the applicant or applicant's spouse may drop out of the labor force and have an interruption of income due to childbearing.
- use unfavorable information about a spouse or former spouse when an applicant applies for credit independently and can demonstrate that the unfavorable history should not be applied.
- discount part-time income (but may examine probable job continuity).
- with certain exceptions, terminate credit on an existing account because of a change in an applicant's marital status without evidence that the applicant is unwilling or unable to pay.

Flood Disaster Protection Act

The **Flood Disaster Protection Act** requires the purchase of flood insurance as a

condition of receipt of federal or federally related financial assistance for acquisition and/or construction of a building in a special flood hazard area (SFHA) of any community. Therefore, the FHA, VA and the Small Business Administration (SBA) cannot make or guarantee a loan secured by a building in a SFHA unless flood insurance has been purchased.

Servicemembers Civil Relief Act

The Servicemembers Civil Relief Act was enacted in 2003 to update the Soldiers and Sailors Civil Relief Act. Its purpose is to ease economic and legal burdens on active duty military members and reservists, or members of the National Guard called to active duty, and, in limited situations, dependents of military members. It does not apply to veterans or to obligations incurred while the servicemember is on active duty.
Relief provided by the Act during and after active service includes:

- restricting the maximum interest rate that may be charged on an obligation following a call to active military service;
- providing certain relief related to evictions;
- requiring court approval for a non-judicial foreclosure unless the servicemember agrees to allow the foreclosure; and
- providing protection to a servicemember who obtained a mortgage after entering active duty, but who is not readily available (especially due to an overseas assignment) to defend him against judicial proceedings.

Brain Teaser
Reinforce your understanding of the material by correctly completing the following sentences:

1. Under the _____ theory of mortgages, a mortgage creates a specific voluntary lien against the borrower's property that may be enforced by foreclosure, through which the borrower's rights to the property would be terminated.

2. When the buyer gives the seller a note for the balance of the purchase price plus a mortgage securing the note in return for a deed to the property, the mortgage is called a _____ _____ mortgage.

3. In an adjustable rate mortgage, a payment cap, limiting the amount the monthly payment may increase, may cause _____ amortization.

4. A _____ mortgage uses only personal property as security for a loan, while a _____ mortgage uses both real property and personal property as security for a loan, and a _____ mortgage uses more than one parcel of real estate as security for a loan.

5. The _____ _____ _____ _____ is a law requiring disclosure of credit costs.

Brain Teaser Answers

1. Under the **lien** theory of mortgages, a mortgage creates a specific voluntary lien against the borrower's property that may be enforced by foreclosure, through which the borrower's rights to the property would be terminated.

2. When the buyer gives the seller a note for the balance of the purchase price plus a mortgage securing the note, in return for a deed to the property, the mortgage is called a **purchase money** mortgage.

3. In an adjustable rate mortgage, a payment cap, limiting the amount the monthly payment may increase, may cause **negative** amortization.

4. A **chattel** mortgage uses only personal property as security for a loan, while a **package** mortgage uses both real property and personal property as security for a loan, and a **blanket** mortgage uses more than one parcel of real estate as security for a loan.

5. The **Truth In Lending Act** is a law requiring disclosure of credit costs.

Review — Finance Laws

In this lesson we discuss the legal aspects of financing in a real estate transaction and a number of finance laws.

Mortgage Instruments
In a mortgage transaction there are two instruments given to the lender in return for the loan: a promissory note or a bond and a mortgage (also called deed of trust or trust deed).

Promissory Note
A note provides evidence of the borrower's debt and a promise to repay the debt. It establishes who the borrower and lender are, the debt amount, interest rate, and terms of repayment. Clauses that may be included are:
- a prepayment privilege, or "or more" clause, allowing the borrower to pay all or some of the outstanding principal balance before it is due.
- a prepayment penalty clause within the prepayment privilege clause.
- a lock-in clause prohibiting any loan prepayment for a certain period.
- a late payment penalty provision.
- an acceleration clause, allowing the lender to declare the entire unpaid loan balance due upon default.
- an alienation clause (or due-on-sale clause or call provision), allowing the lender to call the loan due at once and require immediate payment upon sale of the property or to require lender approval of the buyer.
- in commercial loans, an assignment of rents provision, allowing the lender to collect the rents from the tenants in the property in the event of default.

If the lender allows a purchaser to take title to the property with the lien remaining against the property, the purchaser may either assume responsibility for payment or he may take title subject to the existing loan and not be responsible for the payments. If he takes title subject to the existing loan, he would not be responsible for making the loan payments but would lose his equity if the property were foreclosed. If he assumes and agrees to pay the loan, he will be responsible for making the payments.

When notes are sold on the secondary mortgage market, they are often endorsed without recourse so the endorser does not guarantee payment to the purchaser.

Mortgage or Deed of Trust
The mortgage or deed of trust provides security for the loan. In states operating under the lien theory of mortgages, the mortgage or trust deed creates a specific voluntary lien against the borrower's property.

In a mortgage there are two parties: the borrower (the mortgagor) and the lender (the mortgagee). In return for the loan, the borrower gives the lender a note, promising to repay the loan, and a mortgage, securing the promise. When the loan is repaid, a satisfaction of mortgage is recorded. If the mortgagor defaults, the lender can sue to obtain a judgment or have the property foreclosed. Following a foreclosure sale, the mortgagor may have a right to redeem the property by paying off the debt and all foreclosure expenses. He may be entitled to any amount bid at the sale in excess of the amount needed to pay off the debt and expenses or may be subject to a deficiency judgment for any shortage. At the end of the redemption period, the purchaser will receive a sheriff's deed to the property.

In a deed of trust transaction there are three parties: the borrower (grantor or trustor), the lender (beneficiary), and a third party (trustee). The borrower gives the lender a deed of trust to secure the loan. When the loan is repaid, a deed of reconveyance from the trustee is recorded. If a borrower defaults, the beneficiary may sue to obtain a judgment, foreclose through the court as if it were a mortgage, or have the trustee exercise his power of sale. The power of sale allows foreclosure to be completed much faster than under a mortgage.

Types of Mortgages

A fixed-rate mortgage provides an interest rate that remains fixed for the entire term of the loan. An adjustable- (variable-, renegotiable-) rate mortgage provides for the interest rate to go up or down according to an indicator. A conventional mortgage involves a loan made with real estate as security and not involving government participation in the loan in the form of insuring or guaranteeing the loan. It may be insured by a private mortgage insurance company. An FHA mortgage involves a loan in which the lender is insured by the Federal Housing Administration against loss in the event of foreclosure. A VA mortgage involves a loan in which the lender is guaranteed against loss by the Department of Veterans Affairs in the event of foreclosure.

A term mortgage or straight mortgage provides for no amortization during the term of the loan, payment of interest only throughout the term of the loan, and a lump balloon payment of the entire principal amount due at the end of the term. A reverse annuity mortgage provides for the lender to pay the borrower funds in a lump sum or in monthly advances and/or through a line of credit. Interest is added to the principal loan balance each month so the total amount owed increases as the interest is compounded.

An amortized loan involves gradual liquidation or extinction of the loan during its term through periodic payments of principal. If fully amortized, the entire loan is paid off during the loan term. Fully amortized options include:
- a level-payment mortgage (where each payment remains the same).
- a graduated-payment mortgage.
- a budget or PITI mortgage.
- a direct principal reduction loan.

If partially amortized, some of the loan is paid off during the term and the rest is repaid in a balloon payment at the end of the term; this loan may be called a balloon mortgage. Like most loans, the PITI mortgage requires the borrower to pay the taxes and insurance to the lender monthly, who will pay them when they are due.

A mortgage is a first mortgage if there are no other mortgages on the property with prior lien rights. A mortgage is a junior or second mortgage if it is subordinate to another mortgage. A subordination clause is often used in the financing of land to enable the borrower to obtain a first mortgage construction loan. A wraparound loan is a type of junior mortgage. It differs from other junior liens in that its face amount includes the amount borrowed on the junior lien plus the amount owed on the first lien. A home equity loan is a junior loan in which the borrower is approved for a specific credit limit based on a percentage of the appraised value of the home less the balance owed on an existing mortgage.

Security agreements, replacing chattel mortgages, make personal property security for a loan. A package mortgage uses both real property and personal property as security for the loan, so the borrower need only deal with one lender and has uniform payments distributed over a longer long term.

A blanket mortgage involves one mortgage that covers more than one parcel of real estate as security. It should have a release clause allowing parcels to be cleared of the blanket lien before the entire lien is satisfied. To assure adequate security remains as the parcels are released, the release schedule requires that a greater percentage of the loan be repaid than the percentage the parcels represent. To show a parcel has been released from the blanket lien, a deed of partial reconveyance or a partial satisfaction of mortgage is recorded.

In a participation mortgage, the lender earns interest plus a percentage of the project's net income or of its ownership in return for granting the loan or for granting concessions, e.g., a higher loan-to-value ratio or a lower interest rate.

With a closed-end mortgage, no additional funds can be borrowed without a new note and mortgage. An open-end mortgage allows the borrower to borrow and reborrow additional funds up to a specified maximum amount without negotiating a new mortgage. One type of open-end mortgage is a construction mortgage. This is designed as a high-interest, short-term loan to finance the cost of labor and materials used during the construction of a new building. Funds are disbursed in a series of installments as work progresses instead of disbursed in a lump sum. A long-term loan used to pay off the construction loan upon completion of construction is called a take-out loan.

When the seller takes back a mortgage (called a purchase money mortgage) as partial payment for the property, the purchaser acquires the title immediately upon closing and the seller is given a lien. That mortgage will have priority over all liens the buyer may place on the property. Another seller financing option is to use a contract for deed (or real estate contract) where the seller provides the same terms of credit to the buyer under a contract that provides for the buyer to receive a deed to the property only after he has paid the full balance of the purchase price. Because the seller (vendor) has the legal title and the buyer (vendee) has only equitable title (the right to get the legal title in the future), this is the least secure method of financing.

Laws Governing Financing

The Truth In Lending Act is a disclosure law designed to ensure that applicants for consumer credit, such as residential mortgage and consumer personal property loans, are given sufficient information so they can easily compare credit cost and terms offered by various creditors. The Act and Regulation Z require that lenders provide a disclosure statement showing all finance charges, late fees and payoff penalties, as well as an annual percentage rate (APR) that shows the total of all finance charges as a percentage of the loan. They also regulate all advertising of consumer credit. A lender may advertise specific credit terms (interest rate, monthly payment, etc.) as a dollar amount or percentage only if he actually offers those terms and includes all of the pertinent terms in the ad.

In an effort to make it easier for consumers to compare key information within loan documentation such as interest rates, closing costs of a loan, monthly payments and loan programs from competing lenders, the Consumer Financial Protection Bureau will be consolidating four separate disclosures into two combined disclosures. This new rule, referred to as TRID (the TILA/RESPA Integrated Disclosure Rule) will be implemented and effective as of October 3, 2015. The first consolidation of forms is that the Good Faith Estimate and the preliminary Truth in Lending Disclosure will be combined into a preliminary disclosure referred to as the Loan Estimate. The Loan Estimate must be given to the buyer no later than three business days after submission of the loan application to the lender. The second form consolidation is that the HUD-1 Form and the final Truth in Lending Disclosure will be merged into a disclosure form known as the Closing Disclosure. The Closing Disclosure will be given to the borrower three business days before the loan is consummated.

The TRID rule has an exemption for those lenders who make five or fewer loans per year. The transactions that are exempted from the requirements set forth in this new rule are Home Equity Lines of Credit, reverse mortgages, cash transactions, commercial purpose loans, mobile home loans and no-interest second mortgages that are made for down payment assistance, and energy efficiency or foreclosure avoidance loans.

The Equal Credit Opportunity Act prohibits creditors from discriminating against a loan applicant on the basis of race, creed, color, religion, national origin, sex, marital status, age, receipt of income from public assistance programs, and the exercise of rights under the Consumer Credit Protection Act.

The Flood Disaster Protection Act (FDP Act) requires the purchase of flood insurance as a condition to receive federal or federally related financial assistance for acquisition and/or construction of buildings in special flood hazard areas of a community.

Financing

Overview

This lesson discusses the role financing plays in real estate transactions. The federal government's role in oversight of financial institutions is covered. Conventional and government insured and guaranteed loan sources and differences are distinguished. The significance of primary and secondary mortgage markets is explained. In addition, calculation of interest and points is simplified.

Objectives

Upon completion of this lesson, the student should be able to:

1. List and give examples of the various sources of real estate financing.
2. Explain why points are charged and how to calculate them.
3. Cite the distinguishing features of conventional loans.
4. Describe the influence of the government in mortgage lending, including the Federal Reserve System, the secondary mortgage market and the Rural Housing Service.
5. Identify the significant elements and differences between FHA-insured and VA-guaranteed loans.
6. Define interest and describe the various methods by which interest is computed.

Mortgage Markets

Financing is the lifeblood of real estate development, sales, investment, brokerage and property management, because most buyers are either financially unable to amass the cash to pay the full purchase price of a property or are unwilling to purchase unless they can borrow most of the purchase price. Quite often, the buyer will rely on the expertise of his real estate agent to direct him to the proper lending source. To provide the needed assistance, the agent must understand mortgage markets and current institutional and governmental practices relating to mortgage financing.

There are two mortgage markets: the primary mortgage market and the secondary mortgage market.

----- PRIMARY MORTGAGE MARKET -----

In the **primary mortgage market** lenders originate mortgage loans by lending funds directly to borrowers. Mortgage loans may be provided by institutional or noninstitutional lenders.

Institutional lenders are regulated financial institutions that accumulate the savings of many individuals and use this money to make loans at rates exceeding the rates paid to their depositors. They are also referred to as financial intermediaries as they are the middlemen between the original source of funds and the borrowers of the funds. They include savings banks, commercial banks, credit unions, and life insurance companies.

Noninstitutional lenders include real estate investment trusts, pension and trust funds, private lenders, finance companies, mortgage bankers and sellers of property. Most of these need not guarantee a return to depositors or investors and are therefore able to loan money on more speculative ventures than are institutional lenders. For example, a noninstitutional lender may help limited partners finance their participation through a non-recourse loan that is secured by their ownership in the venture but provides that they are not personally liable for repayment of the loan.

To obtain a mortgage loan, a person could apply either to a mortgage broker or to a lender directly.

Mortgage Broker
A **mortgage broker** brings borrowers and lenders together for a real estate loan. He will seldom make or service loans for his own account. After a loan is closed, he will not collect payments or handle any other service functions for the lender. His function is to take and process loan applications and arrange for lenders to make the loans. As a result, his transactions involve loans using money belonging to others, not his own money. For his service, he receives a commission or a finder's fee, paid by the borrower. Some mortgage brokers will arrange for the purchase and sale of existing mortgage loans in the secondary

mortgage market, again earning a fee for the service. Occasionally, a lender will even broker a loan when it is unable to provide one requested and earn a fee for the brokerage service.

If seeking a lender as a direct source of financing, a borrower has a number of choices. In the past, there were significant distinctions between these sources. Today, as a result of deregulation of various segments of the financial market, the distinctions are less clear.

Mortgage Banker

A **mortgage banker** (or mortgage lender or mortgage company), originates, finances, and closes mortgage loan transactions, and then sells the mortgages to large investors in the secondary market.

Although a mortgage banker may also provide mortgage brokerage services, the mortgage banker differs from the mortgage broker in that as a mortgage banker he will use his own money to make loans and does not need the consent of anyone else in making the loan. However, the mortgage banker is generally not the ultimate lender. Because mortgage bankers do not hold funds belonging to depositors or investors, they often do not have a large amount of loan funds of their own. They prefer to negotiate loans that are most readily salable in the secondary market. As a result, they are very active in making government-insured and government-guaranteed loans, conventional loans for one- to four-family properties, and large construction and development loans for which they have identifiable purchasers. In many cases, the mortgage banker will make the loan only after obtaining a commitment to purchase the loan from a savings bank, bank, insurance company, Fannie Mae, Freddie Mac or other investor. In other instances, the mortgage banker may make the loan and then sell it to the most suitable lender on an individual case-by-case basis.

> **NOTE:** Fannie Mae and Freddie Mac are agencies created by Congress to promote the secondary mortgage market. They, and similar agencies, will be discussed in more detail later in this lesson.

A mortgage banker in need of funds temporarily, between the time it makes the loans and the time it sells them, may warehouse the loans. **Warehousing** involves assembling loans and pledging them with a commercial bank to serve as security for a line of credit.

Mortgage bankers will often contract with the lending institutions for which they originate loans to service the loans they have sold. Mortgage servicing consists of collecting principal and interest payments due on the mortgage, collecting impounds or reserves for property taxes and insurance, paying the appropriate bills when due, handling problems with late or delinquent payments and, if necessary, foreclosing.

Mortgage companies make money by charging:
- an application fee for securing the application.
- a loan origination fee, generally of 1-2% of the loan amount as its commission for processing the loan package.
- a servicing fee of ¼ to ¾ % of the loan balance each year for servicing the loan.

Financing

Mortgage companies are organized and regulated under state law. However, a major element of control over their activities comes from the investors who purchase their loans and agencies that insure or guarantee their loans.

Commercial Banks

Although they have the greatest amount of assets available of any lenders, **commercial banks** prefer short-term commercial and consumer loans to long-term mortgage loans. Their primary real estate financing activity includes short-term construction loans, interim financing of mortgage bankers, home improvement loans, and home equity loans. Long-term loans for residential properties are usually FHA-insured or VA-guaranteed loans as opposed to conventional loans. Commercial banks are either federally chartered or state chartered. Federally chartered banks are supervised by the U.S. Comptroller of the Currency and must be members of the Federal Reserve System (the Fed). State chartered banks may voluntarily become members of the Fed. All Fed members may borrow funds from a Federal Reserve Bank and must have their depositors' accounts insured by the Federal Deposit Insurance Corporation (FDIC).

Savings Banks

The lending institution most involved in the financing of residential property had been the savings and loan associations. Savings and loans were originally created to encourage savings, or thrift, and home ownership. Savings and loans have almost disappeared, with many being reorganized as **savings banks**. Savings banks invest in real estate loans for single-family properties as well as apartments, shopping centers, office buildings and commercial structures. They may be federally chartered or state chartered.

Life Insurance Companies

Life insurance companies are actively engaged in financing real estate but generally not directly with the borrower. They invest major portions of their assets in long-term real estate loans, normally for large commercial, industrial and apartment projects. If they do get involved in residential loans, it is usually through purchase of FHA and VA mortgages in the secondary market. Insurance companies are usually represented by mortgage bankers, who originate and then service the loans. All insurance companies are state chartered rather than federally chartered.

Others

While **pension funds** invest most heavily in government and corporate securities, many will acquire large blocks of mortgages in the secondary market and originate loans through mortgage bankers and mortgage brokers.

Credit unions specialize in short-term consumer loans but may also provide funds for long-term financing of real estate, equity loans and home improvement loans to their members.

Finance companies specialize in consumer loans but may also make real estate loans, usually second mortgage loans for residential property. Larger finance companies will make loans to finance land development.

Real estate investment trusts (REITs) will invest in construction and land development loans for multi-family or commercial properties.

In rural areas, the **Farm Credit Bank** will make loans to farmers and ranchers for the purpose of buying and maintaining homes or land to be used for farming.

Private individuals, such as investors, relatives of the purchaser, or even the seller of the property, can be a source of financing. A seller may provide financing when the buyer of the property has difficulty qualifying for a loan from a lending institution, or in a tight money market. He can finance a portion of the price by taking back a mortgage on the property or carrying a contract.

To assist the buyer in qualifying for a loan at an interest rate he could afford, the seller may offer to pay discount points for the buyer. **Discount points** are prepaid interest charges, or interest rate equalization factors, used to increase the yield to the lender. They may be paid by the borrower or by the seller or anyone else who is willing to do so for the borrower. One discount point is equal to 1% of the loan amount (1 Point = 1% x Loan).

In tight money markets, lenders may add discount points to their loan fees to increase the amount they will collect immediately and thus increase the immediate return on their funds. Even in normal times lenders will offer loans at different interest rates based on charges of a certain number of discount points; e.g., a 7 % loan with no discount points; a 6.75 % loan with two discount points; or a 6.5 % loan with four discount points.

One discount point will increase a lender's yield by 1.66 % to 1.25 % of interest. By paying 1 point (1% of the loan) up front, a borrower may get a reduction in interest of about 1.25 % for the term of the loan.

Generally, loans from private individuals will be for shorter terms than those offered by institutional lenders and may be at higher interest rates because of greater risks.

Loans originated in the primary market may be conventional or government backed.

PRIMARY MARKET	
Conventional	Uninsured or Insured (Private)
FHA	FHA Insured
VA	VA Guaranteed

----- Secondary Mortgage Market -----

After having made a loan, a lender may:
- hold it and bear the risks associated with long-term financing until the entire debt is repaid.
- use the loan as collateral for loans it needs from other lenders.
- sell the loan to another lender or investor.
- use the loan to back securities sold to investors.

When existing loans are sold or used as collateral for other loans or securities, the transactions are said to occur in the secondary mortgage market. The **secondary mortgage market** is the market in which existing loans are bought, sold or borrowed against. While the primary market originates loans, in the secondary market, lenders and investors will warehouse loans, sell them, or buy and hold them.

Secondary mortgage market lenders and investors buy mortgage or trust deed notes, or securities that they back, as long-term investments in competition with other types of securities, such as government bonds or corporate bonds. Some lenders deal in both the primary and secondary markets; others deal in only one market. Those who deal in only the secondary mortgage market pay another party, often the lender originating the loan, a continuing fee to service the debt or service the loan; that is, collect mortgage payments and handle foreclosures.

The practices of primary lenders are greatly influenced by the desires and demands of the lenders and investors in the secondary market. Because of the secondary market:
- primary lending institutions are able to free the funds they have invested in mortgage loans by selling those mortgages to lenders having capital available for real estate investments.
- funds are redistributed from money-rich areas to money-poor areas and fluctuations in the supply of funds available to meet the demand for mortgage loans are minimized.
- interest rates are stabilized across the country and kept at a lower level than they would be if the supply of funds was limited to deposits on hand in each separate lending institution.

Three types of transactions normally occur in the secondary mortgage market:
1. Mortgage **warehousing**, where a lender, usually a mortgage banker, assembles a number of loans into a portfolio and offers the package as security for a short-term loan or line of credit from another lender, such as a commercial bank. This gives the primary lender funds with which to operate until the loans can be sold.
2. Buying and selling individual mortgage loans.
3. Forming a group or pool of mortgage loans and issuing securities backed by the pool. Purchasers of the securities receive an interest in the pool of loans and are repaid their investment as well as interest on their investment from the mortgage payments received by the lender or investor holding the loans.

Financing

In order to promote the secondary mortgage market for residential mortgages, Congress has created a number of agencies:
- Fannie Mae (originally the Federal National Mortgage Association or FNMA)
- Freddie Mac (originally the Federal Home Loan Mortgage Corporation or FHLMC)
- Ginnie Mae (originally the Government National Mortgage Association or GNMA)

These agencies have no direct contact with the public but instead buy and sell loans and offer their securities through mortgage brokers, commercial banks, savings banks, and others. Approved lending institutions enter into selling agreements with these agencies, in which they agree to originate and service the mortgages they offer for sale within guidelines set by the agencies. In originating the loan, the lenders will use the forms and loan criteria of the agency(ies) to whom they might sell the loan. Loans meeting Fannie Mae and Freddie Mac standards are called **conforming loans** (loans not meeting those standards are called nonconforming loans). Loans for an amount in excess of the maximum Fannie Mae and Freddie Mac loan amount are called **jumbo loans**. When money is tight, Fannie Mae and Freddie Mac will purchase mortgages from the lending institutions, and when mortgage funds are plentiful, they will sell loans to others.

Fannie Mae

The largest investor in the secondary market is **Fannie Mae (FNMA)**. FNMA was originally created to buy FHA Title II mortgages to keep the market for FHA loans liquid and stabilize the mortgage market by increasing the amount of money available for credit financing of housing. Today, Fannie Mae's primary responsibility is to maintain an active secondary market for mortgages. To do this, it purchases FHA and VA mortgages and conventional fixed and adjustable-rate first and second mortgages secured by one- to four-family homes. Lenders wishing to sell loans to Fannie Mae will pay a fee to Fannie Mae for a commitment that Fannie Mae will purchase a certain dollar volume of loans at a certain yield over a specified period of time (e.g., 90 days, 180 days, etc.). These may be loans that have not yet been made, as well as loans currently in the lender's portfolio.

Under the Fannie Mae mortgage-backed securities plan, lenders may sell a pool of mortgages in exchange for a like amount of securities (called **participation certificates**) that represent individual interests in the pool of loans. The lender may keep the securities or sell them to investors. Mortgage payments received from the mortgagors, less servicing costs and certain fees, are passed through to those holding the securities. Fannie Mae will guarantee full and timely payment of principal and interest to those holding the securities.

Fannie Mae was originally a government agency, then became a quasi-public corporation owned by private shareholders, and today is again a government agency. It obtains its capital by borrowing, selling long-term notes and bonds in the capital markets, issuing and selling its own common stock, from earnings from its mortgage portfolio and fees, and from the sale of its mortgage-backed securities.

Ginnie Mae

In 1968, when Fannie Mae was rechartered as a private corporation, Congress created the Government National Mortgage Association, today known as **Ginnie Mae**, to administer support programs for FHA, VA and RHS mortgages which could not be carried out in the private market.

Ginnie Mae is a government corporation within HUD. It has three major activities:
1. Manage and liquidate a portfolio of federally owned mortgages
2. Provide special assistance functions, such as financing support for urban renewal projects, housing for the elderly, below-market mortgage risks and experimental housing projects, for which financing is not readily available
3. Guarantee pass-through securities privately issued by approved financial intermediaries (These securities are backed by pools of FHA, VA or RHS mortgages.)

Freddie Mac

In 1970, Congress created the Federal Home Loan Mortgage Corporation, today called **Freddie Mac**, in order to provide a secondary mortgage market for members of the Federal Home Loan Bank System (primarily savings and loan associations). Today Freddie Mac is authorized to buy mortgages from all types of lenders. It purchases mostly conventional mortgages but will also purchase FHA and VA loans. Like Fannie Mae, Freddie Mac issues and guarantees mortgage-backed securities secured by loans in its portfolio.

While these are the major participants in the secondary market, they are not the only ones. Any lender or investor may purchase mortgages directly from primary market lenders.

When loans are sold in the secondary mortgage market, the purchaser may pay the seller the amount owed on the loan, or more or less, depending on the interest rate and whether it is fixed or variable; the time remaining until the loan will be paid off; and the yield or return the purchaser desires. A loan sold for more than the outstanding balance because its interest rate is above current market rates is said to sell at a premium. Selling loans for less than the balance (at a discount) is called **discounting**.

> **For Example**
> A person buying a fixed rate loan of 6% cannot collect more than 6% from the borrower, but he can obtain a higher yield by buying the note at a discount. If he paid $9,000 for a note with a balance of $10,000, he would still receive 6% interest calculated on $10,000 plus the full $10,000 principal. If he has to foreclose, he may sue for the entire unpaid balance owed, rather than the amount he paid. The extra interest and $1,000 additional principal produce the higher yield.

Conventional Loans

Conventional loans are loans made by private parties and nongovernment lending institutions without any government insurance or government guarantee against loss for the lender.

Conventional loans may be uninsured or insured. One factor affecting a lender's risk of loss is the amount of the borrower's down payment. A lender could reduce his risk by requiring a substantial down payment. When a buyer cannot afford such a down payment, the lender may require mortgage insurance. Generally, a conventional loan of up to 80% of the property's value will be made without mortgage insurance. To compensate for the greater risk when the loan is above 80% of the value, some lenders charge higher interest rates, but most require that the loan be insured by a private mortgage insurance company. The borrower pays the insurance premium for the policy that insures the lender against loss in the event of a foreclosure. The premium and the insurance stop once the loan is paid down to 80% of the value of the property at the time the loan was taken. In the event of a default, the insurance company will either pay off the loan or let the lender foreclose and pay the lender for its loss.

Conventional loans differ from government-backed loans in that conventional loans will generally offer the borrower lower loan-to-value ratios, resulting in higher down payments. A **loan-to-value ratio** (LTV ratio) represents the amount of a loan expressed as a percentage of the appraised value or the purchase price of the property, whichever is less.

The loan-to-value ratio formula is: Loan = % x Value or Price (whichever is lower).

> **For Example**
>
> A property has sold for $500,000 and had been appraised at $505,000. A 95% loan would amount to $475,000 (95% of $500,000).
>
> If the property had sold for $500,000 and had been appraised at $490,000, a 95% loan would amount to $465,500 (95% of $490,000).

To calculate a loan, multiply the lower of the price or value by the loan-to-value ratio.

> **For Example**
>
> A buyer wants to make an offer of $190,000 on a property. He has $6,000 available as earnest money. His lender will issue a 95% loan. The property is appraised at $192,000.
>
> Loan = 95% x $190,000 sales price (since that is less than the appraised value) = $180,500. The earnest money does not affect the calculation of the loan, since it is applied to the down payment.

Often, an agent will be told the maximum loan amount for which a client can qualify and be quoted interest rates for 80%, 90% and 95% loans. To determine the prices of the properties that can be purchased at those ratios, he can use the same loan-to-value ratio formula as before: Loan = % x Value

However, since he would know the loan amount, he would divide it by the loan-to-value ratio to find the value.

> **For Example**
>
> If a buyer can qualify for a $467,200 loan and wants to get a 95% loan:
> $467,200 loan = 95% x value
>
> Divide $467,200 by 95% to get the value of the home. This is $491,789.

To determine the loan-to-value ratio itself, divide the loan by the value (or sales price, if lower).

> **For Example**
>
> A buyer can qualify for a $467,200 loan and wants to buy a $491,790 property:
> $467,200 loan = % x $491,790 value
>
> The loan-to-value ratio will be $467,200 divided by $491,790, or 95%.

In summary, to find the loan amount, multiply the value by the ratio; but, if the loan amount is known, divide it by the ratio to get the value, or divide it by the value to get the ratio.

Loan-to-Value Ratio: Loan = % x Value or Price (lower)		
To find loan	Loan	= % x Value or Price
To find value or price	V or P	= Loan ÷ %
To find %	%	= Loan ÷ Value or Price

Conventional loans generally have lower loan-to-value ratios than government-backed loans, such as FHA, VA and Rural Housing Service-insured and guaranteed loans. In addition, conventional loans will generally have due-on-sale clauses if they are fixed-rate loans, and may have prepayment penalties. Government-backed loans are fully assumable by qualified buyers and do not have prepayment penalties.

----- GOVERNMENT-BACKED LOANS -----

The federal government has had a significant impact on mortgage financing through programs provided by the Federal Housing Administration, the Department of Veterans Affairs and the Rural Housing Service (RHS). By and large these programs do not involve loans made by the government agency and do not involve funds provided to lenders by the government agency. Except for a direct loan program by the RHS, the  government programs involve federal insurance or guarantees of real estate mortgage loans that protect lenders from losses caused by default in payment by borrowers and eventual foreclosure. An **FHA loan** is a loan in which the lender is insured by the Federal Housing Administration against loss in the event of foreclosure. The FHA does not serve as a lender and is not the mortgagee. Instead, private lenders, approved by the FHA, are the mortgagees. If the lender agrees to give a loan meeting the requirements set forth by FHA, FHA will insure the loan.

A **VA loan** is a loan in which the lender is guaranteed against loss by the Federal Department of Veterans Affairs in the event of foreclosure.

Federal Housing Administration

The **Federal Housing Administration (FHA)**, a division of HUD, was created in 1934 with the goal of stimulating new jobs in the construction industry, stabilizing the real estate market, and facilitating the sale of new and existing homes. It did this by agreeing to insure qualified private lenders against loss in the event of foreclosure, caused by borrower defaults, if their loans met specifications and the property met minimum property standards imposed by FHA. Through its programs, FHA has encouraged homeownership by making financing of housing affordable to many and increased the quality of housing by requiring improvements to meet minimum housing standards.

Since FHA only insures loans, a person wanting an FHA loan must apply to a lending institution approved by the FHA. The lender will have the property appraised to determine its value and condition. The appraisal will include a description of deficiencies that will require correction prior to FHA approval. This appraisal results in a conditional commitment stating the value of the property and the amount of loan that may be insured if the property and borrower satisfy FHA qualifications. If analysis of the applicant's qualifications indicates he is qualified for the loan, the lender may make the loan. The sales agreement must include an escape clause allowing the buyer to withdraw from the transaction without penalty, if the property appraises for less than the sales price.

FHA insures loans as authorized by Title I and Title II of the National Housing Act. Title I loans include loans to finance repairs, improvements or alterations of existing residences. Title II loans are those loans used to buy or build housing, including single-family, condominium, cooperative and multifamily housing.

The most popular of the FHA loan programs has been the 203b program. This program helps finance the purchase of a one- to four-family home that the borrower will occupy as his residence, using a 15- or 30-year loan and a very small down payment (3.5%). Most loans have a 30-year term even though the total interest paid will be higher, because the monthly payments will be lower.

As with other loan programs, the borrower will generally:
- pay for the appraisal.
- pay an interest rate negotiated with the lender.
- pay a loan origination fee as an initial service charge.

Further, he:
- may pay a commitment fee to lock in the interest rate for a period of time.
- may pay discount points to lower the interest rate.

FHA does not regulate the interest rate, discount points or commitment fees but does limit the loan origination fee for some of its programs.

The borrower (mortgagor) will pay a **mortgage insurance premium** (MIP) to FHA. An upfront premium of 1% is payable when the loan is made but can be financed by adding it to the loan. There is also an annual premium charge, 1/12 of which is collected for FHA by the lender with each monthly mortgage payment. Both premiums are used by FHA to cover losses resulting from the insurance claims submitted by lenders.

FHA has more liberal criteria for loan qualification than what is used for conventional loans, making it easier to qualify for the loan. After the loan is made, the borrower may prepay the loan at any time without penalty. He may also have another person assume his loan. If his loan was originated prior to December 15, 1989, it can be assumed by anyone on a **blind assumption** (without qualification by the lender). If it was originated after December 15, 1989, it may be assumed only by a person who intends to occupy the property as his residence and who is approved by the lender.

Federal Department of Veterans Affairs

The **Federal Department of Veterans Affairs (VA)** loan program was created to assist veterans in purchasing homes. A VA loan is available only to an eligible veteran, reservist, or National Guard member to finance a home he intends to occupy. The loan may be used to buy or build a one- to four-family home, including a townhouse or condominium unit, improve a home, refinance an existing home loan, or buy a manufactured home and/or lot on which to place such a home.

VA loans are not made by the VA. They are made by private lending institutions. Although these institutions are not directly regulated by the VA, they do need VA approval to participate in the program. The VA will guarantee the lender against loss on a portion of the loan if the borrower defaults and the lender must foreclose. The guarantee is 25% of the loan or the current Fannie Mae/Freddie Mac conforming loan limit,

whichever is less. In the event of foreclosure, the VA will pay the lender up to the amount guaranteed. The lender would lose money only if it could not sell the property for the difference between the amount owed and the guarantee. In the case of a $200,000 debt with a $50,000 guarantee, the lender would suffer a loss if he could not recover $150,000 from the sale of the foreclosed property.

To get a loan, the veteran must obtain a **certificate of eligibility** from the VA, showing the amount of guarantee to which he is entitled. Although the VA does not establish loan limits, most lenders require that the amount of the guarantee entitlement plus the cash down payment equal at least 25% of the lesser of the property value or sales price. This means a veteran could borrow up to four times his entitlement without any down payment. He could borrow more with a 25% down payment for the additional amount. Although a veteran cannot transfer an existing loan to other property, when he pays off an existing VA loan or has an eligible veteran assume his loan, he can obtain another VA loan.

The veteran takes his certificate of eligibility to a lender approved by the VA. The lender then processes his loan application and has the property appraised by a VA-approved appraiser. This appraisal results in a **certificate of reasonable value (CRV)**, which establishes the maximum loan the lender may make. The veteran may purchase a property for more than the CRV amount but must pay the excess in cash. He cannot borrow the cash to pay more than that amount so secondary financing is rarely used. Any sales agreement contingent on obtaining a VA loan must have an escape clause allowing the veteran to cancel the sale without penalty if the CRV is less than the purchase price.

If the veteran qualifies for the loan, he must also certify that he will occupy the property as his principal place of residence. If the loan is to acquire a two-, three- or four-family dwelling, the veteran must live in one of the units.

As with an FHA loan, the lender may charge a borrower whatever interest rate, discount points or commitment fees they agree to and may charge up to 1% as a loan origination fee. In addition, the borrower will be charged a funding fee either in a lump sum or as an addition to the loan. This fee is paid to the VA to cover the cost of the guarantee program. The borrower cannot be charged any mortgage brokerage fees or escrow fees. In a transaction financed with a VA loan, the seller will pay the full escrow fee, whereas in other transactions the fee is usually split between the buyer and seller.

As with FHA loans, liberal criteria are used in qualifying an applicant, there is no prepayment penalty, and the loan may be assumed. A loan made prior to March, 1988, may be assumed on a blind assumption. One that was made after that date may be assumed by any veteran or nonveteran who might meet the lender's qualifications. The original borrower would remain liable for the loan unless the new borrower agrees to assume full liability for the repayment of the loan and the lender and VA issues a release of liability.

Rural Housing Service (RHS)

The **Rural Housing Service (RHS)**, formerly known as the Farmers Home Administration, was established primarily to make and insure loans to farmers and ranchers unable to secure credit from other sources. Among its programs, the RHS has made financing available in rural  areas for the purchase, repair and rehabilitation of housing occupied by low-to-moderate-income families and senior citizens. For low-income borrowers, RHS offers a direct loan program through which it subsidizes a part of the mortgage payments. For moderate-income borrowers, the RHS has a guaranteed loan program similar to that offered by the federal VA. Under this program, the borrower obtains a loan of up to 100% of the property value from a private lender and pays a funding fee so the RHS will guarantee the lender against loss resulting from default by the borrower.

----- SUBPRIME LOANS -----

Subprime loans are ones made to people who may have difficulty maintaining the repayment schedule. These loans typically have higher interest rates and less favorable terms in order to make up for higher credit risk.

The term "subprime" refers to the credit quality of borrowers, who have below par credit histories and are considered at greater risk of defaulting on a loan than prime borrowers. Much of the decision as to who is a subprime borrower is based upon their credit report. Subprime borrowers have credit ratings that might include:
- excessive debt
- limited debt
- failure to pay debts completely, or
- a history of late or missed payments
- a lack of credit history

Lenders' standards for determining risk might also consider the size of the new loan, and also take into account the way the loan and the repayment plan is set up: if it is a line of credit, conventional loan, a mortgage loan, interest only repayment loan, or other type of instrument.

----- NON-CONFORMING LOANS -----

The **Office of Federal Housing Enterprise Oversight** (OFHEO) sets the criteria on what constitutes a conforming loan limit that Fannie Mae and Freddie Mac can buy. The criterion includes debt-to-income ratio limits and documentation requirements. The maximum loan amount is set based on the October-to-October changes in median home price, above which, a mortgage is considered a jumbo loan, and typically has higher rates associated with it. In general, any loan which does not meet guidelines is a non-conforming loan.

This is because both Fannie Mae and Freddie Mac only buy loans that are conforming to sell to the secondary market, making the demand for a non-conforming loan much less than conforming loans. It is more difficult for lenders to sell non-conforming loans, thus these loans tend to cost more to consumers, (typically 1/4 to 1/2 of a percent increase in the interest rate.)

Financing

Mortgage Lending Procedures

The first step in obtaining a mortgage loan is to apply for the loan, indicating the purpose and amount of the loan, rate of interest, and terms of repayment desired.

The lender will then begin a mortgage evaluation, or a review of the application. In this process, he will consider a number of factors.

He will look at value of the collateral, i.e., the property offered for security. The lender is concerned with the current value of the property and the trend of values in the neighborhood. The appraiser sent out is not concerned with the loan or the borrower, only with the property. The lender also wants a preliminary title report on the property, in order to have assurance regarding the quality and quantity of the title. He also wants data on taxes, zoning, assessments, income produced by the property, expenses, etc. The type of property is also considered by the lender in establishing loan-to-value ratios. Industrial property usually has the lowest loan-to-value ratio since the use of the property may be highly specialized.

The lender will look at information on the applicant, including his credit, to determine the risk of default. For most lenders, this is the most important consideration. However, some lenders, including predatory lenders, will make loans without regard to the borrower's ability to pay. **Predatory lending** is the extension of credit to borrowers who cannot afford the credit on the terms being offered, with features designed to "strip away" or reduce the borrower's equity in the collateral and increase the likelihood of foreclosure.

In reviewing the credit of the applicant, the lender will analyze his capital, capacity, and character:
- Does he have the capital (down payment) necessary to obtain a loan? The down payment required will depend on the property offered as security, as well as the purpose and type of the loan. The greater the loan-to-value ratio, the greater the risk to the lender. Requiring a larger down payment would reduce the LTV, and therefore reduce risk to the lender.
- Does he have the capacity to repay the loan? The lender will look at his employment record: The longer he has been at one job, the better. The lender will also look at other income, including a spouse's income.
- What is his character, or credit worthiness? The most difficult aspect to evaluate is the applicant's willingness to repay the loan. To help evaluate this aspect, the lender considers credit reports showing the borrower's history of paying past debts and his credit score. The credit score is a rating of how the applicant has handled his credit. Scores closer to 800 indicate excellent credit and result in favorable terms. Those closer to 600 or below indicate poor credit and result in higher interest rates, higher down payments, or rejection of the application.

An important component in the review of the loan application is an analysis of the applicant's **qualifying ratios**, or debt-to-income ratios. One of these, the front-end ratio, relates total housing costs (principal, interest, taxes and insurance) to the borrower's gross income. This ratio should not exceed 28%. The back-end ratio relates long-term debt (such as a car payment and housing costs) to total gross income. This should not exceed 36%. However, lenders will have programs that allow higher ratios, perhaps with higher interest rates, for those with **compensating factors** (i.e., aspects of a person's financial situation that provide a reason to go outside the normal guidelines for making a loan, such as evidence of an ability to afford the payments, a better-than-average credit history, a high credit score, job security, etc.).

----- INTEREST -----

Factors Affecting the Cost of Borrowing

After the applicant's credit has been evaluated and the property has been appraised, the lender can determine the loan amount and terms and issue a firm commitment. Lenders have a great deal of flexibility in establishing loan fees, interest rates, loan-to-value ratios, and maturity dates for loans. The key factors for them are whether they can realize a profit on the loan and whether they have some degree of assurance that the loan will be repaid.

Among the factors affecting the cost of borrowing money (i.e., loan fees and interest rates) are:
- supply and demand. When the demand is greater than the supply, the cost goes up. When it is less than the supply, the cost goes down. The interest rate on real estate mortgages will in part be determined by competition for the use of funds between the money market (the market for loans of one year or less) and the capital market (the market for loans of over one year). Supply and demand is also affected by the general business economy or real estate market. The real estate market is generally subject to more extensive oversupply and undersupply as it tends to lag significantly behind the general economy.
- local factors such as the level of employment, population growth, government restrictions, climate, and the level of development in the community.
- the lender's costs and profit margin. The lender charges a loan origination fee to recover the costs of establishing a new loan. He charges interest for use of the money, accruing as of the disbursement of the funds. The interest rate must cover the cost of obtaining the money, paying for administrative costs and overhead, and providing a profit.
- the degree of risk involved with the loan. The higher the risk, the higher the rate charged.
- yields demanded by investors in the secondary mortgage market. If investors in the secondary market are expecting yields of 8%, a lender in the primary market will have to charge more than 8% if he intends to sell the loan.
- government activity, e.g., usury laws, fiscal policy, and monetary policy.

Usury

State **usury laws** may specify the maximum rate of interest that may be charged for various types of loans in the state.

Fiscal and Monetary Policy

The government attempts to check inflation and deflation. These efforts will affect interest rates on mortgage loans. **Inflation** occurs when there is more money to spend on a limited number of available items. As demand for these items pushes their price up, the result is a decrease in the purchasing power of the dollar. This will cause investors to place their money into equity assets such as real estate, which typically experience an increase in their prices in times of inflation, to reflect the loss in value of the dollar. When there is **deflation**, the purchasing power of the dollar is increased because there are more goods in relation to the money available for buying them.

The government has two policies at work to control inflation: fiscal and monetary.
- **Fiscal policy** is action by Congress to increase or decrease income taxes. To slow the economy and halt inflation, Congress can increase income tax rates, limiting the amount people can spend or save. To stimulate the economy, the government can lower taxes to give people more money to spend, save or invest.
- **Monetary policy** is regulation of the supply and flow of money and credit available in order to promote economic growth with stability. Monetary policy is controlled by the Federal Reserve System.

The **Federal Reserve System (the Fed)** monitors economic and financial conditions, such as the volume of bank deposits and withdrawals, the cost of money and credit, unemployment levels, inflation rates and world economic conditions, and applies various controls or pressures to influence the supply of money and credit available in the economy.

To achieve its goals, the Fed uses three basic tools:
1. Reserve requirements
2. Discount rates
3. Open market operations

The Fed establishes **reserve requirements** for all member banks. Member banks must set aside and keep a certain percentage of their assets as reserves. When the Fed increases its reserve requirements, banks have less money to lend, interest rates rise and borrowing and spending slow down. When the Fed decreases the reserve requirement, banks have more money to lend, causing interest rates to decrease and borrowing and spending to increase. Generally, the Fed makes changes in reserve requirements only as a last resort, since even minor changes have a dramatic impact on the money supply.

The Fed will loan money to member banks to enable those banks to have adequate funds in reserve. The interest rate the bank pays the Fed for these funds is the **discount rate**. The Fed may decrease the discount rate to encourage bank borrowing and reduce bank expenses so that banks are able to lend more money at lower interest rates. The Fed might increase the discount rate when it wants to discourage bank borrowing and decrease the supply of funds banks have available to lend.

Financing

Open market operations refers to the purchase and sale of U.S. Treasury securities, such as Treasury bills and notes. This is perhaps the most flexible and frequently used tool of the Fed for expanding or slowing the economy. The Fed, through the Federal Reserve Bank of New York, trades securities almost daily in order to influence the availability and cost of money and credit. When the Fed buys government securities from the public, it stimulates the economy because the cash paid to the sellers is deposited into the sellers' bank accounts. This increases the banks' reserves, allowing the banks to extend more credit to borrowers. However, if the Fed is selling securities, buyers will withdraw funds for payment from their banks, decreasing reserves in their banks, making less credit and lending available through the banking system. This activity also affects the federal funds rate. This is the interest rate a bank with surplus reserves will charge for an overnight loan to a bank needing additional funds to meet its reserve requirement.

To limit the expansion of the economy and put the brakes on inflation, the Fed might:
- sell government securities.
- raise reserve requirements.
- raise the discount rate.

In times of a tight money market, money would be in short supply and interest rates would be high. This will force many potential buyers out of the housing market or cause them to delay purchasing in anticipation of rates going lower. This creates a buyer's market in which there are more sellers than buyers.

To stimulate the economy by relieving a tight money market and encouraging banks to reduce interest rates, the Fed might:
- buy government securities.
- lower reserve requirements.
- lower the discount rate.

MONETARY POLICY		
Federal Reserve	**Tight Money**	**Inflation**
Open market operations (securities)	Buy	Sell
Discount rate (not prime rate)	Lower	Raise
Reserves	Lower	Raise

Interest Rates
Simple vs. Compound Interest
Interest may be simple or compound. **Simple interest** is interest paid only on the principal owed. **Compound interest** is interest paid on accrued (unpaid) interest as well as on the principal owed. For most real estate loans, the interest charged is simple interest.

> **For Example**
>
> A borrower who owes $100,000 would be charged interest on the $100,000. When he pays $1,000 of principal to reduce the principal balance to $99,000, the next interest charge will be based on $99,000.

The basic **simple interest formula** has three components: interest, rate, and loan balance. The formula is:

Annual Interest = Rate x Loan Balance

To calculate annual interest, multiply the loan balance by the interest rate. Therefore, to calculate annual interest on a $20,000 loan at 9% interest, multiply $20,000 by 9%.

Annual Interest = Rate x Loan Balance
 = 9% x $20,000
 = $1,800

If the loan were a straight loan for five years, one could determine the total interest for the five years by multiplying $1,800 by 5. This would be $9,000.

To calculate the interest for one month, divide the $1,800 annual interest by 12. This is $150. To calculate the daily charge, divide the annual interest by 365. This is $4.93. When the amount of interest is known, the loan balance can be determined by dividing the annual interest by the rate.

Annual Interest ÷ Rate = Loan Balance

> **For Example**
>
> A borrower paid $50 interest for one month on a loan with an interest rate of 10%. To find the loan balance, first convert the monthly interest to an annualized figure by multiplying by 12.
>
> 50 x 12 = $600. Then divide $600 by 10%. This is $6,000.
> Annual Interest ÷ Rate = Loan Balance
> $600 (50 x 12) ÷ 10% = $6,000

When you know the interest paid and the loan balance, you could find the interest rate by dividing the annual interest by the loan balance.

Annual Interest ÷ Loan Balance = Rate

> **For Example**
>
> A borrower paid $1,700 interest on a straight note in one year on a $20,000 loan. The rate would be determined by dividing $1,700 by $20,000. It would be 8.5%.
>
> Annual Interest ÷ Loan Balance = Rate
> $1,700 ÷ $20,000   = .085

Financing

You can determine the length of time a loan has been in effect if you know the total interest paid, the rate and the time. Calculate the annual interest by multiplying the rate by the loan. Then divide the total interest paid by the annual interest to get the number of years the interest has been paid.

> **For Example**
>
> You paid $6,300 at 10% interest on a $10,000 loan.
> Annual Interest = Rate x Loan Balance
> = 10% x $10,000 = $1,000
>
> $6,300 Total Interest ÷ $1,000 Annual Interest = 6.3 years
> 6.3 years x 12 months = 75.6 months

Nominal vs. Effective Rate of Interest

A **nominal interest rate** (named interest rate) is the rate of interest stated in the loan documents. An **effective interest rate** is the rate the borrower is actually paying; it is commonly called the annual percentage rate (APR).

> **For Example**
>
> A note may show a rate of 6% but this rate may be compounded quarterly to produce a return to the lender of $6.14 per $100. Therefore, 6% would be the nominal rate and 6.14% the effective rate.

Fixed vs. Variable Rates

Interest rates for real estate loans may be fixed or variable.

A **fixed rate** will remain the same for the term of the loan, regardless of future changes in the money supply, rate of inflation or anything else. Particularly during periods when the interest rates are relatively low, borrowers will select the fixed-rate loan over a variable-rate loan.

The drawbacks of a fixed-rate loan are that:
- the rate is usually higher than the initial variable rate being offered at the same time.
- if interest rates were to decrease during the term of the loan, the borrower would have to refinance the loan, incurring new loan costs, in order to be able to take advantage of the lower rates. As a result, during periods of high interest rates, borrowers generally will avoid such loans.

Loans with **variable interest rates** are called adjustable-rate loans or **adjustable-rate mortgages (ARMs)**. The interest rate in such a loan may be adjusted at periodic intervals during the term of the loan, based on a predetermined formula tied to an index. The index is a published rate or yield approved by a government agency regulating the lender, such as a Federal Reserve discount rate, U.S. government bond yields, a consumer price index, or the yield on short-term Treasury bills.

So that borrowers will not get locked into a loan they cannot afford, ARMs have a maximum percentage rate (cap) the interest can increase each year and a maximum total increase in rate over the life of the loan. Some ARMs can be converted to fixed loans after a certain amount of time. Borrowers should carefully compare interest rate caps and other features before selecting a loan.

> **Brain Teaser**
>
> Reinforce your understanding of the material by correctly completing the following sentences:
>
> 1. In the _____ mortgage market, lenders originate mortgage loans by lending funds directly to borrowers.
>
> 2. Mortgage _____ is the process of assembling a number of loans into a portfolio and offering the package as security for a short-term loan or line of credit from another lender, such as a commercial bank.
>
> 3. _____ loans are loans made by private lenders without government insurance.
>
> 4. _____ lending is the extension of credit to borrowers who cannot afford the credit on the terms being offered with features designed to increase the likelihood of foreclosure.

Brain Teaser Answers

1. In the **primary** mortgage market, lenders originate mortgage loans by lending funds directly to borrowers.

2. Mortgage **warehousing** is the process of assembling a number of loans into a portfolio and offering the package as security for a short-term loan or line of credit from another lender, such as a commercial bank.

3. **Conventional** loans are loans made by private lenders without government insurance.

4. **Predatory** lending is the extension of credit to borrowers who cannot afford the credit on the terms being offered with features designed to increase the likelihood of foreclosure.

Review — Financing

In this lesson we discuss financing.

Mortgage Markets
There are two mortgage markets: the primary mortgage market and the secondary mortgage market.

Primary Mortgage Market
In the primary mortgage market, lenders originate mortgage loans by lending funds directly to borrowers. The loan may be originated by the lender or through a mortgage broker. A mortgage broker arranges loans with lenders but does not make loans using his own money and does not collect payments for the lender after the loan is made. Lenders who originate loans are either regulated financial institutions or noninstitutional lenders. Financial institutions, also referred to as financial intermediaries, include savings banks, commercial banks, credit unions, and life insurance companies. Life insurance companies prefer large, long-term loans on commercial property, and often have mortgage bankers service their loans.

Noninstitutional lenders include real estate investment trusts, pension and trust funds, private lenders, finance companies, sellers of property, and mortgage bankers. Mortgage bankers use their own funds to originate a large number of loans, preferably those readily saleable in the secondary market, so they can obtain funds to make more loans. They service their own loans and, for a fee, service those that they have sold by collecting the monthly payments for the purchaser.

Loans and Financing
In processing a loan application, the lender determines the risk of default (often the most important underwriting consideration) by considering the value of the property offered for security as well as the applicant's capital, capacity, and credit worthiness. When the buyer has little capital for a down payment, mortgage insurance may be required to insure the lender against loss in the event of foreclosure. When the buyer presents a greater-than-normal risk, the lender may charge a higher interest rate and/or require a higher down payment.

Conventional loans are made by private parties and nongovernment lending institutions, without any government insurance or government guarantee against loss for the lender. Such loans may be insured by private mortgage insurers or they may be uninsured. Conventional loans differ from government-backed loans in that they generally offer the borrower lower loan-to-value ratios (causing higher down payments) and often have prepayment penalties. A loan-to-value ratio is the loan as a percentage of the lower of the sales price or the appraised value of the property.

Government Programs

Government programs generally involve federal insurance or guarantees of real estate mortgage loans in order to protect lenders from losses caused by default in payment by borrowers and eventual foreclosure. They include FHA and VA loans.

The Federal Housing Administration (FHA) has been responsible for making financing of housing affordable to many and increasing the quality of housing by imposing minimum housing standards. Included in the costs paid by the borrower for an FHA loan are the appraisal fee and a mutual mortgage insurance premium that goes to FHA to fund the insurance program. FHA loans are made by qualified private lenders, who are insured by FHA against loss caused by borrower defaults. Advantages of FHA loans to a borrower include:
- a loan-to-value ratio set by FHA.
- a limit on the amount of the loan origination fee.
- FHA property standards.
- the ability to have a buyer assume the loan.
- no prepayment penalty.
- an escape clause that allows him to see the appraisal and get a refund of his earnest money if the property does not appraise for the sales price.

The Federal Department of Veterans Affairs (VA) loan program assists eligible veterans, reservists, or National Guard members in financing a one- to four-family home (if he intends to occupy at least one of the units) by guaranteeing the lender against loss on a portion of the loan if the borrower defaults and the lender must foreclose. The veteran is able to reuse the program as long as he has eligibility or reestablishes eligibility by repaying prior loans. To get the loan, the borrower must have a certificate of eligibility from the VA, and the property must be appraised by a VA-approved appraiser. The appraisal results in a certificate of reasonable value (CRV). If the purchase price exceeds the appraised value the buyer must pay cash for the difference or use the escape clause to withdraw from the transaction.

Interest Rates

Interest is charged for use of money and begins accruing when the funds are disbursed. The interest rate is determined by competition in the money (short-term lending) market and the capital (intermediate and long-term) market and must cover the cost of obtaining the money, paying for administrative costs and overhead, and providing a profit. Most real estate loans charge simple interest (interest on only the loan balance). The simple interest rate is the nominal rate, or the rate specified in the note or contract. Loans will have compound interest (interest charged on interest) when the borrower is allowed to pay less than the full amount of interest being charged each month, and the unpaid interest is added to the loan balance. For these loans, the nominal rate would differ from the effective rate as a result of compounding.

The basic simple interest formula has three components: interest, rate, and loan balance. The formula is: Annual Interest = Rate x Loan Balance.

A seller may offer to pay discount points for the buyer to assist the buyer in qualifying for a loan at an affordable interest rate. Discount points are prepaid interest charges used to increase the yield to the lender. They are considered interest rate equalization factors, as the lender's yield will be the same whether he charged a higher rate without the points or a lower rate with the points. They may be paid by the borrower, the seller, or anyone else who is willing to do so for the borrower. One discount point is equal to 1% of the loan amount.

The Federal Reserve Board (the Fed) affects interest rates through its activities to control the money supply. To stop inflation, the Fed might raise reserve requirements, raise discount rates (rates it charges its members to borrow money from the Fed), or sell government securities through its open market operations. To stimulate a tight money market and make rates lower, it could lower reserve requirements, lower discount rates, or buy government securities.

Secondary Mortgage Market

The secondary mortgage market is the market in which existing loans are bought, sold or borrowed against. Using loan portfolios as security for a loan is called warehousing. Because of the secondary market, primary lenders are able to free the funds they have invested in mortgage loans, fluctuations in the supply of funds are minimized, and interest rates are stabilized across the country.

When loans are sold, they may be discounted. Discounting means buying or selling the loan for less than its current balance, so the buyer can get a return higher than just the interest on the loan.

In order to promote the secondary mortgage market for residential mortgages, Congress created:
- the Federal National Mortgage Association (today called Fannie Mae).
- the Federal Home Loan Mortgage Corporation (today called Freddie Mac).
- the Government National Mortgage Association (today called Ginnie Mae).

Fannie Mae is a quasi-public institution whose primary responsibility is to maintain an active secondary market for residential mortgages. Fannie Mae and Freddie Mac purchase insured and noninsured conventional loans, as well as FHA and VA loans, and issue and guarantee mortgage-backed securities secured by loans in their portfolio. Ginnie Mae guarantees pass-through securities privately issued by approved financial intermediaries and backed by pools of FHA, VA or Rural Housing Service mortgages, used for special housing purposes (such as housing in urban renewal projects, housing for the elderly, and experimental housing).

Oregon Finance

Overview

This lesson begins with an explanation of the differences between the mortgage, the trust deed and the land sales contract in Oregon, including their methods of foreclosure. It concludes with a discussion of the Oregon VA loan program.

Objectives

Upon completion of this lesson, the student should be able to:

1. Explain the significant differences between a mortgage and a trust deed.
2. Identify various causes of default and remedies for default.
3. Describe how mortgage and trust deed foreclosure procedures differ.
4. Describe the requirements for recording a land sale contract.
5. Identify the legal remedies for default of a land sales contract.
6. Describe the purpose of the state VA loan program.
7. Identify the qualifications for a state VA loan.

Security and Default

----- MORTGAGES AND TRUST DEEDS -----

In a real estate loan transaction, before parting with the funds, the lender will have the borrower sign a written contract **hypothecating** (or pledging) real property he owns, or will own, to secure the debt. This pledge of property to secure the debt would be in the form of a trust deed or a mortgage.

Oregon is a lien theory state. In Oregon, a mortgage or a trust deed will create a voluntary contractual lien, and that lien is a specific lien against the property as security for the promissory note. During the period of the indebtedness, the borrower holds the title, retaining legal ownership while the property is encumbered by the lien.

Because the mortgage and trust deed create a lienholder's interest in real estate, the Statute of Frauds requires that they be in writing and signed by the owner of the property. They need not be signed by a lender or be recorded to be valid between the parties. However, lenders will record them, so they can establish priority of their lien and provide constructive notice of their lien right.

A property encumbered by a mortgage or trust deed may be further encumbered with a second trust deed or mortgage. It may even be sold before the trust deed or mortgage is paid off. The owner may convey title to another by giving that person a deed, unless the mortgage or trust deed includes a provision requiring that he pay off the loan upon the sale or get the lender's approval of the buyer to assume the loan.

While a mortgage and a trust deed serve exactly the same purpose, they differ in two main areas: the number of parties involved and the means by which the lender may foreclose if the borrower defaults. The major difference between the mortgage and trust deed is in the lender's remedies in the event the borrower defaults.

Mortgage

In a mortgage there are two parties: the borrower (mortgagor) and the lender (mortgagee). If a mortgagor defaults, the mortgagee can sue on the note or foreclose through the court by means of judicial foreclosure.

Evidence that a mortgage has been paid in full is a **satisfaction of mortgage** signed by the mortgagee.

Trust Deed

In a trust deed there are three parties: the borrower (grantor), the lender (beneficiary), and the third party (trustee). If a grantor defaults, the beneficiary may sue on the note, foreclose through judicial foreclosure, or foreclose through a trustee's sale. A trustee can only be an attorney, a bank, trust company, or savings and loan association, a title insurance company, a licensed escrow agent, or a federal government agency. The trustee cannot be the borrower or the beneficiary. This is because the trust deed gives the trustee a power of sale, which allows the trustee to foreclose and sell the property on behalf of the beneficiary without the need to go through judicial foreclosure procedures in court.

> **NOTE:** The power of sale is not the legal title to the property. It is only the right to foreclose out of court.

Evidence that a trust deed has been paid in full is a **reconveyance deed**. After a trust deed has been paid in full, the beneficiary is obligated to make a request for reconveyance to the trustee named in the trust deed. In response, the trustee will sign the reconveyance deed and send it to the grantor. When recorded, it removes the lien of the trust deed from the county records.

A mortgage or trust deed can also be released by foreclosure or by sale of the property to the lender resulting in a deed in lieu of foreclosure.

----- DEFAULT -----

Several types of remedies are available to the parties of a financing instrument in the event one or both parties default.

Breach

A **default** is a breach of any of the terms or conditions of a loan agreement. Default may result from any of the following:
- Failure to make the periodic payments specified in the note or contract when they are due
- Failure to obtain the lender's permission to allow the loan to remain in effect prior to alienating the property
- Failure to maintain the property such that its value was seriously reduced
- Removal of improvements from the property
- Sale of a portion of the land without the lender's permission
- Failure pay the amounts due for reserves for taxes and insurance
- Failure to pay for other liens having priority over this one
- Failure to keep an adequate amount of property insurance in force to cover the lien
- Use of the property for an illegal purpose, e.g., in violation of a zoning ordinance
- Misrepresentation on the loan application, such as stating the property would be used as a residence and immediately renting it out, or lying about income, work status, or the like

After a borrower defaults, a lender will consider:
- the borrower's equity in the property.
- the current state of the real estate market.
- the positions of junior lienholders.
- the circumstances causing the default.
- the borrower's attitude and willingness to cure the default.

If the reason for the default is reasonable, the lender can enter into a **forbearance agreement,** or moratorium, with the borrower. In a forbearance agreement, the lender agrees to delay taking legal action in return for the borrower's agreement to satisfy certain arrangements to cure the default. A **moratorium** is a type of forbearance agreement in which the lender waives collection of all or part of the mortgage payments for a reasonable period of time to help the borrower cope with financial difficulties. Once the period is over, the borrower would be required to make up the postponed amounts through higher payments, more payments, or a balloon payment at the maturity date of the loan.

An alternative to forbearance is **recasting** of the loan. This involves rewriting the terms of the loan for the balance owed as a new loan.

If forbearance or recasting is not feasible and the borrower cannot sell the property to pay off the loan or have someone assume his debt, he could voluntarily offer the lender a **deed in lieu of foreclosure**. In the deed (called an **estoppel deed**), the borrower relinquishes all rights in the property in return for the lender's agreement to take no further legal action against him. The deed will state that the loan is in default and subject to foreclosure, the deed is being delivered in order to avoid foreclosure, and the consideration for the deed is full cancellation of the debt and release from further recourse against the borrower. The deed will convey title subject to all existing encumbrances, so the lender will be obligated to handle these as if he were the borrower.

Legal Remedies

If all of these alternatives fail, the lender will issue a notice of default to the borrower so he can seek a legal remedy.

One legal remedy is called rescission. **Rescission** is an agreement between the parties to the contract or a court order to cancel and no longer recognize the validity of the agreement. With a rescission, both parties are restored to the same position as if they had never entered into the contract at all. This would be the remedy when:
- the parties to an installment contract agree that there has been a serious misunderstanding about some element in the contract; or
- when a court declares a contract void on the basis that fraud or misrepresentation improperly induced one of the parties into the agreement in the first place; or
- when a vendor is unable to deliver marketable title to a vendee.

In a rescission, the court may issue a writ of restitution requiring further acts to reduce any harm that has resulted while the contract had been in effect. It may require the vendor to return the vendee's down payment and all of his monthly payments but also require the vendee to pay the fair market rent for the time he occupied the vendor's property.

A second remedy is a **suit for specific performance**. When a vendee defaults on a land sales contract, the vendor could sue for specific performance, request a sheriff's sale of the property if the vendee does not perform, and then obtain a deficiency judgment if the sales proceeds did not satisfy the judgment.

When a borrower fails to pay a mortgage or trust deed note, the lender could sue for a judgment on the basis of the note rather than foreclose on basis of the mortgage or trust deed. This remedy might be used when it appears that the borrower has sufficient capital or other assets to satisfy the judgment or that the property might not sell at foreclosure for the amount owed.

----- FORECLOSURE -----

Another legal remedy is **foreclosure**. By definition, to foreclose means to shut out, bar, exclude, or to deprive of the right to redeem a mortgage or trust deed. It is a procedure designed to terminate a borrower's interest in the property so the lender may acquire the value of the pledged collateral.

Foreclosure and sale is the most common legal remedy to default, as it is the required method of foreclosing mortgages and trust deeds. Foreclosure and sale allows the lender to force the sale of the property by court order or by a trustee's power of sale, with proceeds from the foreclosure sale used to pay off the debt outstanding at the time of default.

Strict foreclosure, which does not involve a sale, is allowed in Oregon only for foreclosure of a land sales contract.

Mortgage Foreclosure

To begin a mortgage foreclosure process, the lender will issue a **notice of default** to the defaulted mortgagor. This is the official notification of the act that constitutes the default and activates the acceleration clause, which declares the entire principal balance and delinquent interest due and payable at once. At that point, the lender has the right to refuse back payments. He may then file a petition with the court to sue for foreclosure and request an order for foreclosure and sale.

Once the suit is filed, it will be placed on the court calendar. When the suit is filed, the mortgagee may ask that a notice of lis pendens be recorded, giving notice of the pending suit and protecting its claim against the property. The lis pendens can be recorded in any county or counties in the state to limit any transactions on other properties owned by the mortgagor in those counties. A title search may also be done to determine the identities of all parties having an interest in the property so notice may be sent to them and they can have the opportunity to redeem the mortgage or appear in court to defend their interests.

When the suit finally reaches court, all parties having an interest in the property, including the defaulted mortgagor, have the right to appear in court and defend their interests.

If the judge grants a foreclosure, he will issue a judgment decree, establishing the total amount owed, including the unpaid loan balance, past due interest, court costs and legal fees, and issue a writ of execution, ordering the sale of the property by an officer of the court, usually the county sheriff. The sheriff will notify all persons with an interest in the property and publish a notice of sale in the local newspaper at least once each week for four consecutive weeks. Prior to the foreclosure, interested parties have an **equitable right of redemption**. This is the right to pay off the debt before the foreclosure.

Usually, the foreclosure sale is at the county court house. It is conducted on an auction basis, with the property being sold to the highest bidder. The sale is on a cash basis, so the high bidder must pay cash to satisfy the debt owed. A cash deposit is normally required at the time of the auction, with the balance due in a few days. If the amount realized at the sale exceeds the indebtedness, the excess is given to the mortgagor. If the bid does not pay off the total owed, the first mortgagee may be able to obtain a deficiency judgment for the amount remaining, but junior liens are wiped out.

Following a judicial foreclosure and sale, the borrower must give up possession of the property but retains legal title until the end of a statutory redemption period. Under the **statutory right of redemption**, the mortgagor, or his heir, devisee, or even a grantee who has acquired the legal title to the property by any other means, can at any time within 180 days after the date of sale, redeem the property, by paying an amount equal to the *total* of the following:
- The amount of the price bid by the certificate holder
- The amount of any property taxes the purchaser may have been required to pay
- Any money necessarily expended by him to prevent waste
- All sums he may have been required to pay on prior liens
- 9% annual interest on every payment made by the purchaser
- *Minus* the amount of rents and profit the purchaser obtained from the property while it was in his possession

At the time of redemption the judge or the court would determine the exact amount necessary to redeem.

Upon payment of the full amount of the bid, the high bidder at the foreclosure sale is issued a **certificate of sale** from the sheriff, showing the price paid for the property, the date of the sale, and his rights. The certificate does not give him title to the property. He has the right to use and possess the property and can live in it or even rent it out. However, he must keep the property in a reasonable state of repair and cannot permit or commit acts of waste. If the property is not redeemed, the certificate holder is entitled to keep the rents and profits earned from the property during the redemption period and will receive a **sheriff's deed**, conveying the title to him.

If the mortgage foreclosed upon was a junior mortgage, the certificate holder's rights are subject to all other prior encumbrances. This means, if he does not make payments on those encumbrances, the prior lienholders would be able to foreclose and take the property from him.

With foreclosure on a mortgage and sale of the property, the lender may have a right to a deficiency judgment against the foreclosed mortgagor for the amount of the deficiency when the sale proceeds do not cover court costs, sheriff expenses, sale expenses and satisfy the entire debt.

This is a personal judgment against the borrower for the balance still owing on the note after a foreclosure sale. This right to a deficiency judgment is a definite benefit to the lender but is not always allowed. It is not available for a junior mortgage or a purchase money mortgage. In Oregon a purchase money mortgage is a mortgage used to finance the purchase of a primary or secondary residence. It is a mortgage:
- given by a borrower to the seller.
- of $50,000 or less.

Trust Deed Foreclosure

The beneficiary of a trust deed may sue on the note for specific performance, giving up his right to foreclose, if he anticipates that a foreclosure sale would not satisfy the debt.

Alternatively, he may foreclose judicially, as if he were foreclosing on a mortgage. As with a mortgage foreclosure, this process allows him, upon default, to accelerate the note and declare the entire amount owed due and payable. However, he must allow the borrower a 180-day right of redemption after the foreclosure sale. The only difference would be that he might not have a right to a deficiency judgment. In Oregon, a beneficiary who forecloses on a nonresidential trust deed by judicial proceedings is entitled to a deficiency judgment. He cannot obtain a deficiency judgment if the trust deed is a **residential trust deed**. A trust deed is residential when it covers real property on which there are four or fewer residential units, one of which is occupied by and is the principal residence of the grantor, the grantor's spouse, or the grantor's minor or dependent child at the time the trust deed foreclosure is commenced.

The most widely used trust deed foreclosure option in Oregon is foreclosure by advertisement and sale, or trustee's sale, because it is much faster than the judicial foreclosure process.

The beneficiary starts the process by notifying the trustee that there has been a default and instructing the trustee to issue, record and send a **notice of default** to the grantor, to the occupant of the property, and to any other person, such as a junior lienholder who would be affected by a forced sale of the property. The notice announces the default and informs the parties that the property will be sold if the default is not corrected.

The trustee must file the notice of default and send it to the affected persons at least 120 days prior to the proposed date of the trustee's sale. The trustee must advertise the sale in a newspaper or a journal of general circulation at least once a week for four consecutive weeks, ending at least 20 days before the date of the sale.

The borrower, his successor in interest, or any person having a subordinate lien may reinstate the loan by paying all back payments, accrued interest on the payments and legal costs incurred, up until five days prior to the sale date. The **right of reinstatement** requires the lender to accept the borrower's offer to cure the default, discontinue the sale proceeding, and reinstate the trust deed as if no foreclosure proceedings had been initiated.

If the loan is not reinstated or redeemed, the trustee will conduct an auction-type sale at which anyone except the trustee may bid, including the borrower and lender. The trustee will apply the sale proceeds to the sale expenses, trustee and attorney fees, and then to outstanding encumbrances in their order of priority. Any surplus is paid to the defaulted grantor. If there is any deficiency, the beneficiary cannot get a deficiency judgment, regardless of whether the trust deed is residential or nonresidential.

The purchaser at the sale receives a **trustee's deed**, giving him legal title to the property without warranties. No certificate of sale is needed, because the borrower does not have a right of redemption following the sale. The purchaser is entitled to possession of the property 10 days after the sale.

Because a trustee's sale is less expensive and faster than a judicial foreclosure, most real estate loan transactions are financed using trust deeds rather than mortgages. However, because mortgages were in use before trust deeds were developed, most financing terminology still uses the word "mortgage" (mortgage company, mortgage market, etc.), even though the documents used today are actually trust deeds, and Oregon is very specific in the Oregon Trust Deed Act (ORS 86.705-86.795) that a trust deed is treated as a mortgage on real property and much of the law that relates to mortgages also relates to trust deeds. The grantor in a trust deed is the mortgagor and the beneficiary is the mortgagee. The main difference between a mortgage and a trust deed is that while a mortgage is foreclosed through the court system, trust deeds are foreclosed non-judicially, or outside of the court system.

Instead of filing a lawsuit in court, a foreclosure is started by filing a "notice of default" and after 120 days have passed, an auction of the property can be held. Once the "notice of default" occurs, Federal law requires a mandatory mediation to be offered to the homeowners to see if something other than foreclosure can be worked out such as a loan modification, a deed in lieu of foreclosure or possibly, a short sale. The mediation is "mandatory" in the sense that the lender is required to offer it to the homeowner and required to participate if the homeowner wishes to do so.

ORS.86-735 of the Oregon Trust Deed Act has been quite controversial in times of high foreclosure rates. The courts have found that the Mortgage Electronic Registry System (MERS) cannot act as a nominal beneficiary and must follow the statute which says that before a non-judicial foreclosure can take place, the assignments of the lender's interest must be recorded in the county of record.

----- LAND SALES CONTRACT -----

In a land sales contract, the vendor holds legal title as security for payment of the purchase price. The contract is valid and enforceable between the vendor and vendee whether or not it is recorded. Because an unrecorded contract would not be valid against future purchasers without notice, however, the contract, or a memorandum of the contract, should be recorded to provide notice of the vendee's interest in the property. Recording will protect the vendee but will not pass legal title to him or affect any prior encumbrances.

A **memorandum of contract** is a separate document used to disclose the existence of the contract without disclosing all of the financial terms of the contract. Recording a memorandum of contract has the same legal effect as recording the contract itself.

In order to provide protection to vendees, Oregon law requires that, when title will be conveyed more than 12 months from the date a land sales contract is executed, the vendor must, within 15 days from the date the parties are bound by the contract, record the contract or a memorandum of the contract. Failure of the vendor to do so will subject him to a fine but will not affect the validity of the contract between the parties. In actuality, recording is usually performed by the escrow agent on behalf of the vendor upon closing. Once the contract has been recorded, if the parties terminate the agreement before the buyer is given a deed, it may be advisable to obtain a quitclaim deed from the vendee, releasing his claim to the property, so he can deliver marketable title to any new purchaser.

A land sales contract will specify which acts constitute default and which remedies the vendor may use to satisfy the default. All remedies, such as rescission, deed in lieu of foreclosure, specific performance, foreclosure and sale and, in Oregon, strict foreclosure are available to be included in the contract.

Strict foreclosure would be used by a vendor who wants to regain clear title to the property rather than have the court force the sale of the property. It requires litigation to ask the court to declare the buyer's interest null and void and to allow the lender to take all rights to the title of the property without a judicial sale of the property.

To begin the foreclosure process, the vendor, through his attorney, issues and records a notice of default, stating that if the default is not corrected the vendor will seek a remedy in court. If the default is not cured, the court will determine whether or not the vendee has actually defaulted on the contract terms and whether or not the contract was reasonable. It may then issue an interim decree (called an interlocutory decree), stating the amount due on the contract.

The vendee is given a specified time (generally 90 days to one year) to pay that amount due before the property would be foreclosed. This right to pay off the debt prior to foreclosure is called an **equitable right of redemption**. If the vendee fails to redeem within the specified period, the court will issue a final decree, foreclosing the vendee's interest in the property and giving the vendor full legal title. From that point, the vendee is allowed no further redemption right.

However, if the judge determines that a vendee's equity interest in the property is substantial, he may order that the vendor return a portion of that interest to the vendee. On the other hand, if the value is less than the amount owed, the vendor would not be entitled to a deficiency judgment against the vendee to recover the loss.

The contract may also have a **forfeiture clause** in the event of default allowing the contract to be terminated without court action with the vendor retaining all payments made by the purchaser. In Oregon, a vendor may have the contract forfeited after allowing the vendee a specified period of time ranging from 60 to 120 days to cure the default, depending on the percentage of the purchase price remaining unpaid.

Oregon Veterans Loan Program

The state of Oregon has a loan program to enable qualified eligible veterans to borrow money from the **Oregon Department of Veterans' Affairs** (ODVA) to acquire an owner-occupied, single-family home in Oregon. The ODVA gets the money to lend from the sale of tax-exempt bonds and loans it out at an interest rate based on the rate it pays to bondholders. The bonds are paid off from the money collected from the veterans' mortgage payments.

To get the loan, the veteran must reside in Oregon at the time of application, be buying a home in Oregon and be an honorably discharged veteran who served on active duty:
- for at least 210 consecutive days (unless released earlier because of a service-connected disability), or
- for less than 210 consecutive days but served in an area for which a campaign or expeditionary medal was authorized.

He must apply for the loan within 30 years from the date of release from active duty.

To qualify for the loan, the veteran must give the ODVA a copy of his military separation report (Form DD-214) and an eligibility application. He must get from the ODVA an eligibility certificate, listing the maximum amount he may borrow, and take it to the ODVA office or an approved lender to apply for the loan.

The loan must be used to purchase or improve a single-family, owner-occupied primary residence for the veteran. It is at a fixed interest rate set by the ODVA. The maximum term is 30 years. Loans over 80% loan-to-value ratio must be insured. A separate account is established to collect and pay property taxes, property insurance and loan cancellation life insurance if the loan to value ratio is over 80%.

A person may obtain a second ODVA loan to purchase a home for up to the difference between his original loan amount and the current loan maximum, if he has paid off his original loan in full or transferred it to another person. He may have his entire loan right restored and obtain another loan for up to the current maximum loan limit if the original loan has been paid in full or transferred to another and if his original home was:
- destroyed by fire, flood or other natural hazard.
- taken through condemnation.
- lost or disposed of for a compelling reason, through no fault of the veteran (e.g., a job transfer or change of employment to another locality).

Brain Teaser

Reinforce your understanding of the material by correctly completing the following sentences:

1. Because the mortgage and trust deed create a lienholder's interest in real estate, the _____ _____ _____ requires that they be in writing and signed by the owner of the property.

2. Under the statutory right of redemption, the mortgagor can redeem the property at any time within _____ days after the date of sale.

3. A _____ of contract is a separate document used to disclose the existence of the contract without disclosing all of the financial terms of the contract.

Brain Teaser Answers

1. Because the mortgage and trust deed create a lienholder's interest in real estate, the **Statute of Frauds** requires that they be in writing and signed by the owner of the property.

2. Under the statutory right of redemption, the mortgagor can redeem the property at any time within **180** days after the date of sale.

3. A **memorandum** of contract is a separate document used to disclose the existence of the contract without disclosing all of the financial terms of the contract.

Review — Oregon Finance

This lesson covers the differences between the mortgage, the trust deed and the land sales contract in Oregon and the Oregon VA loan program.

Mortgages

In Oregon a mortgage or a trust deed will create a voluntary contractual lien that is a specific lien against the property pledged as security for a promissory note. The mortgage and trust deed must be in writing and signed by the owner of the property. They need not be signed by a lender or be recorded to be valid between the parties.

If a mortgagor defaults, the mortgagee can sue on the note or foreclose through the court by means of judicial foreclosure. In a mortgage foreclosure, the judge issues a judgment decree, establishing the total amount owed, including the unpaid loan balance, past due interest, court costs and legal fees, and a writ of execution, ordering the sale of the property, by an officer of the court, usually the county sheriff. The sale is conducted on an auction basis, with the property being sold to the highest bidder. If the amount realized at the sale exceeds the indebtedness, the excess is given to the mortgagor. If the bid does not pay off the total owed, the first mortgagee may be able to obtain a deficiency judgment for the amount remaining. However, junior liens are wiped out. Upon payment of the full amount bid, the high bidder is issued a certificate of sale from the sheriff. Following the foreclosure sale, the defaulted borrower must give up possession of the property but retains legal title and may redeem the property within 180 days after the date of sale. If the property is not redeemed, the certificate holder will receive a sheriff's deed.

Trust Deeds

A trust deed gives the trustee a power of sale so he can foreclose and sell the property on behalf of the beneficiary without the need to go through judicial foreclosure procedures in court.

If a grantor defaults, the beneficiary may sue on the note for specific performance. He may foreclose judicially, after accelerating the note and declaring the entire amount owed due and payable. However, he must allow the borrower a 180-day right of redemption after the foreclosure sale. If he forecloses on a nonresidential trust deed by judicial proceedings he is entitled to a deficiency judgment. A trust deed is residential if it covers real property on which there are four or fewer residential units, one of which is occupied as the principal residence of the grantor, the grantor's spouse, or the grantor's minor or dependent child at the time the trust deed foreclosure is commenced.

The most widely used trust deed foreclosure option is foreclosure by advertisement and sale, or trustee's sale, because it is much faster than the judicial foreclosure process. The beneficiary notifies the trustee that there has been a default. The trustee must file the notice of default and send to the affected persons at least 120 days prior to the proposed date of the sale, and advertise the sale at least once a week for four consecutive weeks ending at least 20 days before the date of the sale. The borrower, his successor in interest, or any person having a subordinate lien may reinstate the loan by paying all back payments, accrued interest on the payments and legal costs incurred, up until five days prior to the sale date. If the loan is not reinstated or redeemed, the trustee will conduct a sale. This is an auction at which anyone except the trustee may bid at the sale, including the borrower and lender. Any surplus is paid to the defaulted grantor. If there is any deficiency, the beneficiary cannot get a deficiency judgment. The purchaser at the sale receives a trustee's deed, giving him legal title to the property without warranties. The borrower does not have a right of redemption following the sale. The purchaser is entitled to possession of the property 10 days after the sale. A trustee's sale is less expensive and faster than a judicial foreclosure.

After a trust deed has been paid in full, the beneficiary is obligated to make a request for reconveyance to the trustee, who will sign the reconveyance deed and send it to the grantor. When recorded, it removes the lien of the trust deed from the county records.

Land Sales Contract

In a land sales contract, the vendor holds legal title as security for payment of the purchase price. The contract is valid and enforceable between the vendor and vendee whether or not it is recorded, but an unrecorded contract would not be valid against future purchasers without notice. To protect the vendee, when title will be conveyed more than 12 months from the date a land sales contract is executed, the vendor must record the contract or a memorandum of the contract within 15 days of the contract. Strict foreclosure is allowed in Oregon only for foreclosure of the vendee's interest in a land sales contract.

Oregon Veterans Loan Program

Qualified eligible veterans may borrow money from the Oregon Department of Veterans' Affairs (ODVA) to acquire an owner-occupied, single-family home in Oregon. The veteran must reside in Oregon at the time of application, be buying a home in Oregon, be honorably discharged after serving the required amount of time on duty, and apply for the loan within 30 years from the date of release from active duty.

A person may obtain a second ODVA loan to purchase a home for up to the difference between his original loan amount and the current loan maximum, if he has paid off his original loan in full or transferred it to another person. He may have his entire loan right restored and obtain another loan for up to the current maximum loan limit if the original loan has been paid in full or transferred to another and if his original home was destroyed by fire, flood, or other natural hazard; taken through condemnation; or lost or disposed of for a compelling reason, not his fault (e.g., a job transfer or change of employment to another locality).

Real Estate Appraisal and Investments

Overview

In this lesson we explore the process of developing an opinion of real property value. Basic economic principles are reviewed. The duties of an appraiser are outlined, including three approaches to estimating current value of a given piece of property: sales comparison, cost and income. The lesson concludes with a review of the elements of real estate investment, with the advantages and disadvantages of selecting real estate as an investment option clarified.

Objectives

Upon completion of this lesson, the student should be able to:

1. Define the concepts of an appraisal.
2. Explain the primary purpose of state licensing and certification of appraisers.
3. Explain the difference between an appraisal and a market analysis (CMA).
4. Explain the differences between market value, market price and cost.
5. Explain why the value of real property does not remain constant.
6. Define the three approaches to value and give examples of the general use of each: sales comparison, cost and income.
7. Explain the concept of highest and best use.
8. Explain the basic concept of depreciation.
9. Explain the difference between reproduction cost and replacement cost.
10. Explain the disadvantages, advantages, and purposes of real estate as an investment.
11. Define the terms "leverage," "equity," "basis" and "capital gain."
12. Describe the purpose and effect of tax deductions and tax credits.
13. Describe the tax benefits of real estate investment, depreciation, installment sales, and exchanges.

Valuation of Real Property

----- VALUATION AND APPRAISAL -----

Valuation is the act or process of developing an opinion of value by anyone. A real estate appraisal is an appraiser's opinion of value resulting from the analysis of facts. An appraisal is not a determination of value, only an opinion.

Licensing Appraisers

The federal **Financial Institutions Reform, Recovery, and Enforcement Act (FIRREA)** of 1989 requires that a real estate appraisal used in connection with a federally related transaction be performed by a person licensed or certified by the state. A **federally related transaction** is a real estate-related financial transaction involving a federal agency or a financial institution regulated or insured by a federal agency. Many states have further expanded the licensing and certification requirement at the state level to apply to any real estate appraisal, even if it is not for a federally related transaction.

To qualify for licensing or certification, a person must satisfy experience, education, and examination requirements set by the state under guidelines adopted by The Appraisal Foundation, a national organization composed of the major appraisal organizations.

A **state licensed appraiser** is a person licensed to make appraisals of:
- noncomplex one- to four-family residential units having a value of less than $1,000,000.
- complex one- to four-family residential units having a value of less than $250,000.
- nonresidential property having a value of less than $250,000.

A **state certified residential appraiser** is a person certified to make appraisals of:
- all types of residential property of one to four units without regard to transaction value or complexity.
- nonresidential property having a value of less than $250,000.

A **state certified general appraiser** is a person certified to make appraisals of all types of real property, regardless of value.

Appraisal vs. CMA

In an appraisal, a licensed or certified appraiser will develop an opinion of value by using a number of different appraisal approaches and then reconciling the results to arrive at the opinion of value.

A real estate agent will present his opinion of value in order to assist the owner in setting a listing price or the buyer in making an offer. This opinion of value is called a **competitive** (or **comparative**) **market analysis (CMA)**. It relates the subject property to similar properties that have recently sold and properties that are currently available for sale.

A market analysis is a method of determining the price for which the subject home should sell based on what purchasers have paid for homes with similar features and in the same general neighborhood.

Usually, agents are able to price residential property in minutes with the aid of computer databases and software programs. However, the computer searches of multiple listing service data and the analysis of the results of the search do require an understanding of some basic concepts of value.

While a market analysis is not as comprehensive or technical as an appraisal and does not consider all relevant approaches to estimating value, it is very similar to one of the approaches (the sales comparison approach) and does call for the real estate agent to apply a number of valuation principles.

Value, Price, and Cost

Value is worth. **Value** relates to the relationship between an item desired and a potential purchaser for the item, rather than to the item itself.

> For Example: A $.15 pencil to the manufacturer may be worth $.05; to a wholesaler, it may be worth $.07; to a retailer, it may be worth $.10; to the purchaser, it may be worth $.15. However, if that person has pencils at home but needs one for only a few hours, it may be worth $.05. If that pencil is needed by a person who has paid $100 to take an exam and forgot a pencil and he will forfeit the $100 unless he can get a pencil, a pencil may be worth almost anything. Therefore, the value of that pencil would vary from person to person and from time to time.

Subjective and Objective Value

Value can be subjective or objective. **Subjective value** (also called utility value, value in use, or investment value) is value related to the use for a specific user even if there is no identifiable open market demand for the item.

> For Example: Schools, churches, libraries, single-use factories, industrial facilities, and company headquarters would be appraised for a specific use value. Their value would not be based on activity in the rental or sales market but on the contribution of the property to the utility or profitability of the owner.

When buyers are willing to pay more or invest more in a property than they know they would be able to realize on resale, the value to them reflects a subjective value. **Objective value** (also called value in exchange or market value) does not relate to just a specific user. Based on the **willing buyer/willing seller concept**, **market value** may be defined as the most probable price a property should bring in a competitive and open market under all conditions necessary for a fair sale, assuming that the buyer and seller are each acting prudently and knowledgably and that the price is not affected by undue stimulus (e.g., special financing or sales concessions).

Real Estate Appraisal and Investments

Market value is determined by buyers and sellers, not by appraisers. Appraisers can only give opinions as to what that value might be.

Price and Cost

Market value is not the same as market price or cost. Because the conditions for market value do not apply to every real estate transaction, the actual amount paid for a property will be its **price** (or market price). Price and value differ when parties:
- are not equally motivated (e.g., the buyer has subjective reasons for wanting the property).
- are pressured to buy or sell (e.g., there is a pending foreclosure).
- are not well informed or are victims of misrepresentation or high-pressure sales tactics.

> For Example: There is a beautiful tree on a slope. The shade from the tree is ideal. The view from near the tree is pristine. The price to put a roadway around the tree would be higher than the cost of felling the tree and putting in a straight driveway. The owner does put the roadway around the tree. The tree could be said to have economic value much higher than the value of the lumber from the tree added to the savings from cheaper construction.

Cost is the total amount of money, labor, material and services spent to produce or develop the item. It does not necessarily reflect or control value.

> For Example: The cost of constructing a house includes the cost to buy the land, put in streets and utilities, and construct the building. If the structure were built competently and reflected current tastes, and there was a normal market for that property, the value may very well be based on the builder's costs plus reasonable profit.

Characteristics of Value

Differences in value are caused by the four characteristics of value:
1. Utility
2. Scarcity
3. Effective demand
4. Transferability

Utility is the ability to satisfy a need or desire of a potential buyer. Land in an urban growth boundary has utility to a builder as the source of buildable lots, but land outside the urban growth boundary would lack such utility for a builder.

Scarcity is also needed. An item cannot have value unless there is also a degree of scarcity. As long as fresh air is plentiful, there is no demand to buy it, and it has no commercial value. Because of scarcity, value is influenced by supply-and-demand factors. Property with a view sells for more than property without a view because of scarcity. If every property in an area had a view of the mountains, there would be no additional value for the view.

Effective demand is demand for the item from people with a desire or need for it and the purchasing power to acquire it. The greater the desire or need for an item of those able to translate the desire/need into a purchase, the greater the potential value. A buyer may want a $2,000,000 house, but without the necessary funds, that desire would not influence the sale price of that house.

Transferability refers to the fact that, if benefits of an item are not transferable, the item has no value to a prospective purchaser. If property available for sale includes only a life estate, fewer rights are capable of being transferred and it will have a lower value than a fee estate.

PHYSICAL AND ECONOMIC
----- CHARACTERISTICS OF REAL ESTATE -----

Certain physical and economic characteristics unique to real estate affect its use and value.

Physical and Economic Characteristics
There are three basic physical characteristics of real estate:
1. Immobility: The location of any given parcel of land cannot be changed. The major factor affecting real property value is its location. This results in relative scarcity of usable land. The choices and preferences for a given area (called "situs") causes similar parcels in different locations to have different values.
2. Indestructibility: Land may lose value and may change its appearance, but it generally does not disappear, unless there is a natural disaster.
3. Non-homogeneity or heterogeneity: No matter how similar it may be to others, each parcel has its own location and features (e.g., size, shape, topography).

These characteristics result in real estate markets being local in character. Furthermore, adjustments relating supply to demand in a real estate market usually occur slowly, resulting in real estate cycles of oversupply (buyers' markets) followed by undersupply (sellers' markets) and back to buyers' markets again.

General Forces
Real estate values are also affected by four **general forces**:
1. Physical and environmental characteristics, which can encourage or prevent development: Physical characteristics include any manmade or natural aspects of the location that make the location desirable or undesirable (e.g., schools, shopping, transportation). Environmental considerations include climate, hazards (e.g., earthquake, hurricane, flood), topography, natural barriers to growth (e.g., rivers, mountains), soil, view, water, etc.
2. Economic conditions, which cause property values to increase or decline: These include current employment and wage conditions, trends in interest rates and availability of mortgage money, building costs, etc.

Real Estate Appraisal and Investments

3. Governmental or political regulations: These include direct tax levels, zoning, and growth and environmental limitations.
4. Social influences: These result in increased values for properties catering to the needs of an incoming population and decreased values for those properties catering to needs of the exiting population. Social influences on real estate values include population growth or decline and trends in population composition (e.g., influx or exodus of the elderly, families with children, and singles).

Any increase in value resulting from these forces, which are outside the influence and control of the property owner (e.g., from favorable rezoning, inflation or population growth), is considered an **unearned increment**.

Building construction in the United States is identified by either the International Building Code (IBC) or the Insurance Services Office (ISO). Both of these organizations classify construction types based on their resistance to fire. The most common types are:

- **Frame buildings**: This is the type of construction used in most homes. They are buildings with exterior walls, floors and roofs of combustible construction. Wood frame is the most typical in residential construction.
- **Joisted Masonry buildings**: These are buildings with exterior walls of masonry or fire-resistive construction. There are several types of joisted masonry buildings:
    - Brick
    - Concrete
    - Hollow concrete blocks
    - Tile
    - Stone

Light Noncombustible buildings are buildings with exterior walls of light metal or other noncombustible material, and noncombustible floors and roofs. These are typically steel frame buildings.

There are a wide variety of possible material combinations, for all classifications of buildings.

Residential homes are usually constructed with concrete or concrete block foundations, wood framing, wood subfloors, drywall interior walls, wood or concrete based siding, and asphalt shingle or steel roofing. A contractor's construction schedule for a home might look like this:

- Excavate for foundation
- Pour footings
- Pour foundation walls
- Rough framing of home
- Utility installation (electric, gas, water, sewer lines, etc.)
- Install roof
- Siding installation
- Insulation installation
- Drywall installation on interior walls
- Finish carpentry including door and cabinet installation

Real Estate Appraisal and Investments

- Window and door trim work
- Countertop installation
- Tile floors and bath walls installation
- Appliances installation
- Light fixtures installation
- Finish heating, plumbing and electrical work
- Install carpet and hardwood floors

Homes are built using a variety of styles. Some of the more typical styles found in most neighborhoods are:

- **A-frame**: This style features steeply angled sides that also serve as the roof. The roof begins on both sides of the rectangular house and meet at the top in the shape of an "A".
- **Bungalow**: These are typically 1 or 1 ½ story homes with a sloping roof and exposed rafter tails. One might consider the bungalow as the forerunner of the ranch style.
- **Cape Cod**: These houses originated in New England and are characterized by their 1 ½ stories, steep roofs, gables and a central chimney.
- **Craftsman**: Sometimes called the Arts and Crafts style is an American original. This style features clean lines and the use of natural materials with a usually almost square floor plan a large, sometime wraparound front porch and front and side gables. This style is found in many older neighborhoods.
- **Colonial**: This is really almost not a style in itself, but is represented by a variety of different building styles. It date back to very early America and can be a simple home or an elaborate style such as the Dutch Colonial with its full front porch and elaborate columns.
- **Mid-Century Modern**: This is a relatively new style that describes of lot of housing built from the 1940's through the early 1960's. These home are found in 1950's neighborhoods and are usually a one level with very clean and sharp lines.
- **Ranch**: A ranch home is usually one level with a close to the ground profile. This home is found in many suburbs of cities.
- **Split-Level or Tri-Level**: These homes have floors levels that are staggered and the main level of the house is halfway between the upper and lower floors. Another variation is the Split-Entry which has the central stairway located at the front door which is halfway between the upper and lower floors.
- **Victorian**: These homes were built during the reign of Queen Victoria (1837-1901) and are characterized by steep pitched roofs and very ornate decorative features.

----- ECONOMIC CONCEPTS AND PRINCIPLES -----

The characteristics of real property lead to certain economic concepts and principles relating to the valuation of real property.

The principle of **anticipation** holds that value is created by the expectation of future benefits to be derived from ownership and use of the property. While a buyer might take into account past sales and recent sales prices of similar or comparable properties, he would base his offer on what he thinks is the current value of the benefits he will derive in the future. This is the basic principle behind the appraisal of income property: The appraiser attempts to estimate the present value of income to be received in the future.

Whenever one makes comparisons, one is applying the principle of substitution. The principle of **substitution** holds that the value of property that is replaceable tends to be set by the cost of acquiring an equally desirable substitute property without any undue delay. This principle is the basis for all appraisal approaches: the sales comparison approach, the cost approach, and the income approach.
- **Sales comparison approach** (market data approach): In this approach, homes and land are valued by comparing prices paid for similar properties.
- **Income approach**: In this approach, properties which produce rental income (e.g., office buildings, apartments, retail properties) are valued based on their anticipated net income and rate of return. The appraiser will base the rate of return on rates received by investors who purchased similar properties.
- **Cost approach**: The cost approach is most commonly used when sales data is lacking for the sales comparison approach and rental data is insufficient for the income approach (e.g., in appraising a church or a single-use property). In this approach, the appraiser compares the existing property to a similar building to be built. He estimates the value of the land, the cost to replace the improvements on the land, and the depreciation that makes the improvements as they exist less desirable than new improvements.

The principle of **change** holds that value estimates are valid only as of a specific point in time as neighborhoods and properties tend to go through a four-stage life cycle:
1. Integration (development or growth)
2. Equilibrium (stability or maturity)
3. Disintegration (deterioration, decline or old age)
4. Revitalization or rehabilitation

The principle of **conformity** holds that maximum value is realized when there is a reasonable degree of architectural homogeneity (or similarity) and land uses are compatible and conform to the standards for the area. Placement of ultramodern homes next to Victorian-style homes or extensive mixtures of residential and commercial uses would indicate a lack of conformity.

Underimprovements, overimprovements and misplaced improvements are those improvements that lack conformity with their surroundings. This leads to two related concepts:

- **Regression**: This concept holds that the value of better property will suffer if it is placed in an area of lesser valued homes. The value of a home built at a cost of $250,000 would suffer if placed in an area of $160,000 homes.
- **Progression**: This concept holds that the value of a lesser property will be enhanced if it is placed in an area of better homes. The value of a home built at a cost of $250,000 would be enhanced if placed in an area of $400,000 homes.

The principle of **supply and demand** holds that an increasing supply of units or a declining demand for them adversely affects the price they can obtain on the market. A decreasing supply or increasing demand would have the opposite effect. In a buyer's market, the supply of houses available exceeds the demand. In a seller's market, the demand for houses exceeds the supply and prices go up. Remember, demand must include buying power to satisfy the desire for a property.

The principle of **increasing and diminishing returns** holds that the value of property is governed by the contribution made by the four agents of production (i.e., land, labor, capital and coordination). The last agent to be satisfied is the land. Therefore, after the costs of labor, capital (money) and coordination (management) are paid, the remaining value is the value of the land. There are increasing returns as larger amounts of these agents produce greater net benefits. However, once the maximum value of the property has been reached, any further increase in these agents would not produce enough of a return to justify the additional investments.

> **For Example**
> After an owner with a $170,000 home spent $3,000 for improvements that added $10,000 in value, he spent another $5,000 for improvements that added $8,000 in value. He then spent another $6,000 for improvements that added $5,000 in value. Initially, he had increasing returns on his investments in his home, but as he added more improvements, the percentage of increased value diminished, until the last set of improvements did not increase the property value by even the amount spent.

The principle of **competition** holds that profits will encourage competition, and excess profits tend to create excessive competition, which can destroy profits.

The principle of **contribution** holds that the value of an improvement is measured by its contribution to the net return of the property (i.e., whether the money spent would add value in excess of the cost and at an acceptable rate of return). This would apply in determining whether to convert a basement to an apartment or whether to install a swimming pool in an apartment complex.

One aspect of contribution is the ratio of the land to the building area. An example is that a 10,000 square foot building site that has a 2,500 square foot home on it would have a **land to building ratio** of 4:1. This becomes important in determining if the land is being used in a comparable ratio to the properties surrounding the subject property, and whether the land is being put to its **highest and best use**.

The maximum value of land exists when the property is used for its **highest and best use** (i.e., the use that at the time of the appraisal is most likely to yield the greatest net return over a given period of time). This return could be measured in money or in the form of amenities. **Amenities** are aspects of a location or design that make the property more desirable (e.g., fireplaces, proximity to shopping and schools, building style, etc.)

Under the principle of highest and best use only those uses that are legal, possible, probable and economically feasible can be considered. Public and private restrictions dictate what uses are legal or permissible. When both apply, the more stringent restrictions prevail, whether they are public or private.

> **For Example**
> As the use of property is limited by zoning and private restrictions, the highest and best use of land zoned for a single-family dwelling cannot be a 20-unit apartment building; and the highest and best use of land zoned for 20 units is not a single-family home.

Depending on the circumstances, increased value may result from dividing large parcels into smaller ones or from creating greater utility by putting several parcels together. Putting several parcels of land under one owner is called **assemblage**. The added value resulting from assemblage is called **plottage.**

> **For Example**
> Two lots, each 100' wide, can only be used to place houses on them. As a result they are worth $40,000 each, or $80,000 total. When put under one owner, the result is a parcel 200' wide, which is large enough for a fourplex. Because of the greater possible utility, the two lots are worth a total of $140,000 together. This is $60,000 more than the total value when they were separately owned. This increase in value is plottage increment.

The Appraisal Process

An **appraisal** is an opinion of value or the act or process of developing an opinion of the value of a property, or an interest in a property, as of a specified date by a person skilled in the analysis and valuation of real estate (an appraiser). The result of this process is usually a written appraisal report setting forth the estimate of value and any reservations or limiting conditions that apply to it.

In its Uniform Standards of Professional Appraisal Practice (USPAP), the Appraisal Foundation shows the real property appraisal process as an eight-step process:
1. Define the appraisal problem
2. Conduct a preliminary analysis and develop a plan, and select and collect data
3. Develop a highest and best use opinion
4. Develop indicators of land or site value
5. Develop indicators of improved property value
6. Analyze prior sale, current agreements, options or listings of the subject property
7. Reconcile the value indicators to reach an opinion of value
8. Report opinion(s) of value

Market Analysis

Depending on the appraisal assignment, general data and a market analysis may or may not be needed.

General data includes characteristics of the region, city and neighborhood, gathered primarily through research. Appraisal of the specific parcel entails a neighborhood analysis, since the location of the property is the primary factor affecting its value.

Specific data regarding the property being appraised relates to:
- construction costs, sales prices, rental rates and operating expenses of properties comparable to the one being appraised.
- title information.
- legal and physical factors influencing the land value (e.g., zoning, property taxes, use restrictions, easements, and information about the site and improvements).
- the improvements.

The **Uniform Residential Appraisal Report (URAR)** divides the description into the following categories: general description, exterior description, foundation, basement, insulation, room list, interior, heating, kitchen equipment, attic, amenities, car storage, and comments.

The general description is necessary to ensure that the proper structures are selected for comparison.

Depreciation

In analyzing the improvements, the appraiser must be aware of the depreciation of the improvements. **Depreciation** is defined as a loss in value from any cause. It results when improvements begin to lose acceptability to prospective purchasers or renters.

In some appraisals, the appraiser looks at depreciation from the standpoint of what has happened and in others from the standpoint of what is likely to happen. The loss in value from what has happened is accrued depreciation. **Accrued depreciation** is the difference between the value of the building at the time of the appraisal and the current replacement cost of the structure in new condition.

> **NOTE:** The land does not depreciate; only the improvements (buildings, sidewalks, cultivated orchards, etc.) do. From the moment they are added to the land, they begin to lose value in relation to their cost if new.

> **For Example**
> A house originally cost $100,000 to build. Today it is worth $450,000. If it burned to the ground, it would cost $600,000 to replace. This house has depreciated, since the $450,000 would be less than the cost of replacing that house with a new house today. The accrued depreciation for this structure, the difference between the replacement cost and the current value of the structure, would be $150,000.

In looking ahead to future depreciation, the appraiser considers **accruals for depreciation**. When an investor purchases income-producing property, his concern is with the depreciation he will have to correct out of income received from the property in the future. The investor wants to be sure that income received would be sufficient to recover the loss due to depreciation and leave a profit.

Depreciation results from physical deterioration and obsolescence.

Physical deterioration is the wear and tear or breaking down of the physical structure, which takes place over time. It is caused by natural forces and by use and may be evidenced by decay, dry and wet rot, insect damage, wear and tear, and vandalism. A major contributing factor is deferred maintenance. Deferred maintenance is usually identified as a lump sum expense needed for overdue repairs. It is best estimated by the appraiser observing the condition of the subject building.

Physical deterioration may be curable or incurable:
14. Deterioration is curable when items are repairable or replaceable and it makes economic sense to repair or replace them (e.g., a broken window or walls in need of paint).
- Deterioration is incurable when the item is not repairable or replaceable or when it would not be economically feasible to repair or replace them at the time. For example, a roof that is five years old may be worth $1,000 less than it would be

worth new, but since it would not be economically feasible to spend any money to replace the roof, the depreciation is incurable.

Obsolescence is the loss in the usefulness of structures that causes them to become less desirable or less useful. Obsolescence is usually more difficult to correct than deterioration. It is outdatedness caused by:
- new inventions, construction methods, equipment, and systems (e.g., plumbing, heating, and electrical).
- changes in the public's preferences (e.g., architecture, location, room sizes, ceiling height, etc.).

Obsolescence may be functional or external (economic).

Functional obsolescence is the loss of value due to factors of inadequacy or overadequacy within the property itself, often caused by changes in construction materials, methods, equipment and the desires of people.
- Factors of overadequacy would include a heating system too large for the house, decorations costing more than buyers are willing to pay for them, or other items exceeding reasonable requirements.
- Factors of inadequacy would include outdated plumbing features and components smaller than normally expected (e.g., a lack of closet space, a four-bedroom home with one bath, a poor room arrangement).

As with physical deterioration, functional obsolescence may be curable or incurable.
- Curable functional obsolescence results from features that are no longer considered desirable by buyers but can be replaced or redesigned at a reasonable cost. It can be estimated by determining the cost to cure.
- Incurable functional obsolescence would be items such as a poor room arrangement or a design feature that could not be corrected without an unreasonable amount of cost. For example, older multistory industrial buildings are less suitable than one-story buildings; this cannot be cured.

External obsolescence (also called **economic obsolescence**) is a loss in value resulting from conditions outside the property. Among the many causes of external obsolescence are deterioration of the neighborhood caused by changes in use of neighboring properties, blight, changes in zoning and legislative restrictions, or fumes from a factory. Since economic obsolescence is external to the property, it is generally incurable.

Depreciation affects an appraiser's judgment of the age and life of the improvements. Each property has an actual physical age and an effective age.
- The **actual age** of improvements is the length of time they have been standing.
- **Effective age** is the age of a similar and typical property of equal usefulness, condition and future life expectancy. It is the age the improvements appear to be, based on their condition. Since the condition of the improvements depends on

how well the property is maintained and whether it has been remodeled or upgraded, the effective age may be less or greater than the actual age.

> **For Example**
>
> A 10-year-old building that is poorly maintained might have an effective age of 15 years, meaning that it is more comparable in utility and condition to a 15-year-old structure than to a 10-year-old structure.

Deterioration and obsolescence limit the usefulness of improvements to a physical life and an economic life.
- **Physical life** is the period of time between the completion of building construction and the time when the building is no longer fit or safe to use. (The physical life of the building is terminated by deterioration.)
- **Economic life** is the period of time between the completion of construction and the disappearance of the building's ability to produce services or income sufficient to offset the expenses. (The economic life is terminated by obsolescence.)

Because physical life represents the time a building can actually stand and economic life represents the time it would be profitable to let it stand, the economic life can never be greater than the physical life. It may be, and frequently is, less.

----- APPRAISAL APPROACHES -----

After gathering data about the neighborhood, site and improvements, the appraiser is ready to develop the value of the property using any or all of the three basic appraisal approaches that may apply to the property:
1. Sales Comparison
2. Cost Approach
3. Income Approach

Sales Comparison Approach

Real estate licensees marketing and selling single-family residences need a good understanding of the **sales comparison approach** (also called the **market data approach**). This is the valuation of properties based on the prices paid for similar, or comparable, properties. Since it is using comparison, it is based on the principle of substitution.

This is generally the best method of estimating the value of any type of property for which there is a sufficient number of sold comparable properties available (e.g., land, residences and other buildings with a high degree of similarity for which a ready market exists).

Real Estate Appraisal and Investments

In performing this analysis, an appraiser will seek properties similar to the one being appraised and gather and verify relevant sales and/or rental data regarding these properties. Sales prices can be obtained from the appraiser's own records, financial news services, multiple listing sources, other appraisers, title insurance companies, and recorded deeds. Most deeds show the actual price paid for the property.

Since no two parcels are exactly alike, each comparable property is compared to the subject property, taking into consideration the following elements of comparison:
- Conditions of sale: The terms and conditions of the sales should be determined to see if they are typical for the market. An atypical sale could involve special financing terms, a buyer and/or seller with inadequate knowledge or extreme motivation, a foreclosure or other forced sale, or a sale to relatives. In some instances, the sales price can be adjusted to account for the sale conditions; in others, such as a foreclosure sale, the sales price is generally not used at all as an indicator of value. The most reliable source of information on the sale price and conditions of sale of a comparable property is often the title company, which can provide a copy of the last recorded deed.
- Date of sale: The sale of each property being compared should be reasonably current. If it is not, an adjustment must be made if market conditions have changed between the date of sale and the date of the appraisal.
- Location: Adjustments are needed to compensate for locational differences. Similar properties would sell for different prices in different neighborhoods or even in a different location in the same neighborhood.
- Physical characteristics: Physical characteristics may be determined by inspection of the properties, MLS data, interviews with a buyer or seller or their agent. Factors affecting value would be style, floor plan, degree of repair, size, room count, lack of a garage, design, view, special features, quality of materials, landscaping or lack of it, and so on. In the appraisal of vacant lots, the zoning must be considered, as only lots of similar zoning should be used.

> **NOTE:** Acquisition cost or purchase price is not relevant in estimating value using this approach.

Differences between the comparable properties and the subject property need to be judged in terms of their probable effect on the price of each sold property and assigned either a dollar or a percentage value.
- Where a difference in the comparable property detracts from its value, the value of that item is added to the sales price of the comparable property.
- Where an element makes the comparable property more desirable, the value of that feature is deducted from the sales price of the comparable property.

By adding and subtracting for differences in the values of these features, the appraiser can obtain an adjusted sales price for each of the comparable properties. This provides a value range for the property being appraised. The appraiser, using his judgment, can then estimate the market value of the subject property within this range. He would not average his figures to arrive at the estimate but would give the greatest consideration to comparable sales that have occurred recently and have the greatest degree of comparability.

Below is an example of how the sales comparison method is used.
- Sales #1 and #3 were bigger houses than the one being appraised. In the appraiser's estimation, the additional size made them worth $10,000 more than the subject property. Therefore, $10,000 is subtracted from the actual sales price of each of the comparables. If Sale #1 had been the same size as the subject property, it should have sold for $10,000 less, or $226,600.
- With regard to condition of the property, Sale #2 was in worse condition than the subject property by $3,200, so $3,200 would be added to its price. If Sale #2 had been in the condition of the subject property, it would have sold for $3,200 more.
- Sales #1 and #2 are adjusted for time (the nine months since their sale) by adding 1% to their sales prices.

	Subject Property	Sale #1	Sale #2	Sale #3
Price Date of Sale Financing Size (Sq. Ft)	2022	$236,600 9 months 90% Conventional 2207 (-$10000)	$222,800 9 months 90% Conventional 2022	$239,800 current 90% Conventional 2207 (-$10000)
Bedrooms Baths Garage	3 2 2	4 2.5 (-$2000) 2	3 2 2	4 2.5 (-$2000) 2
Construction Condition Location	Brick Average Next to Expressway	Brick Same Better (-$3000)	Brick Worse (+$3200) Better (-$3000)	Brick Same Better (-$3000)
Lot Size	90' x 165'	Larger (-$4200)	Larger (-$4200)	Larger (-$4200)
Other Features Time	Patio	Patio +1% (+$2400)	Patio +1% (+$2200)	Patio
Total Adjust		(-$16800)	(-$1800)	(-$19200)
Adjusted Value		($219,800)	($221,000)	($220,600)
Indicated Value $220,500				

Once all the necessary adjustments have been totaled, the appraiser arrives at adjusted values for each of the properties and an indicated value for the subject property. In the above example, only three comparables are shown due to space limitations. An appraiser would generally analyze a larger number but show only three or four in the appraisal report.

Cost Approach

A second method of appraising real property is the **cost approach** (also called the **summation approach, replacement cost approach**, or **reproduction cost approach**). This approach can be used to appraise almost any type of improved property, but as it requires a greater degree of skill than the sales comparison approach, the cost approach is not the preferred method when the sales comparison approach is applicable. The cost approach, therefore, is most commonly used for specialty property such as public buildings, single-use factories, churches, etc. It is also used for evaluating property for fire insurance.

The most difficult aspect of this approach is estimating accurately the depreciation to the property, so the approach may be used where this difficulty is least likely to exist, such as for appraisals of new buildings. This approach is not conducive to appraising older buildings and cannot be used if the highest and best use of the land is different than its current use.

The basis of the approach is that the value of improved property can be estimated by adding the value of the land to the depreciated cost of the improvements on the land. The process involves the following steps to arrive at the current value of the property:
1. Estimate the value of the land.
2. Add the estimated cost of replacing or reproducing the improvements with new ones.
3. Estimate and deduct the depreciation to the improvements.

> **NOTE:** The alternate name "summation approach" is derived from the adding and subtracting in this approach.

Like the sales comparison approach, the cost approach is based on the principle of substitution. It is valid because a person will pay no more for a building than the cost of constructing an equally desirable substitute, assuming no unusual delay.

The first step in the approach is to estimate the value of the land as if it were vacant, generally by using the market data approach. In the cost approach, the land is appraised separately from the improvements.

The next step is to estimate and add the cost to replace or to reproduce the improvements on the property with new ones.
- **Replacement cost** is the present cost of constructing a substitute structure equal to the existing structure in quality and utility but using current construction methods, materials, design and layout.
- **Reproduction cost** is the present cost of constructing a substitute structure that is an exact replica of the existing structure, i.e., with the same materials, quality of workmanship, design and layout. Since reproduction cost might involve estimating the costs of utilizing materials and construction practices that are outmoded, it would be impractical or even impossible to estimate in many instances; reproduction cost would generally be used only for unique properties. Most often replacement cost, the cost of an equally desirable substitute, is used.

Whether based on reproduction or replacement, the cost desired is today's cost of replacing the existing improvements with new ones, not the actual cost of the existing structure itself. A home that cost $4,000 to build 30 years ago, might cost $200,000 to replace today with a new structure with similar utility and amenities. The $200,000 figure would be the one sought.

Among the methods commonly used to estimate cost are the comparative cost method, the unit-in-place method, and the quantity survey method:

- The **comparative cost method** (also known as **square-foot method** or **cubic-foot method**) is fast, inexpensive, and easy to understand, so it is the one most commonly used. It involves comparing the subject property with other similar buildings whose costs are known. Those costs, when divided by the number of square feet (for residential property) or cubic feet (in some commercial property) in the building, provide a unit cost per square foot or per cubic foot. This unit cost, when multiplied by the number of square or cubic feet in the subject property, produces the replacement cost.

> **For Example**
>
> The building being appraised has 1,500 square feet. The cost of similar buildings is $80 per square foot. The replacement cost would be 1,500 x $80 or $120,000. Adjustments would be made for the costs of various exterior and interior features that differ from the norm.

- The **unit-in-place method** is a modification of the quantity survey. It involves combining all the costs into a unit cost for each portion of the building installed (or "in place"). Costs of floor structure, appliances, framing, stairway, heating, plumbing, roof, and foundation generally are based on this method.
- The **quantity survey method** is the most detailed and complex of the methods and most frequently used by builders and professional cost estimators as the basis for a bid on a construction contract. It involves a complete itemization of all direct costs (e.g., hours of labor, cubic yards of concrete, etc.) and indirect costs (e.g., office overhead, insurance, interest, permits, contractor's profit, etc.).

Information about costs can be obtained from local contractors, professional cost estimators and building cost reporting services.

If the building is the highest and best use for the land, and the land value and reproduction cost, or the replacement cost of new improvements, have been properly estimated, the total of the land value and the cost new will yield the upper limit of value of the property. (Land + Cost New = Upper Limit of Value). This upper limit is the property's maximum value, not the current market value.

Depending on the depreciation of the improvements, the market value may or may not be close to this upper limit of value. The current market value will be derived after the next steps in the approach: calculating accrued depreciation and then deducting it from the upper limit.

Calculating accrued depreciation entails measuring the loss of value that has already occurred over the past life of the improvement. A number of methods may be used to do this, depending upon the sophistication required. The simplest, though least accurate, is the **straight-line (age-life)** method. This method is based on the presumption that the improvements depreciate at an equal rate each year until the end of their economic life, when the building would be torn down.

Since the building loses 100% of its cost over its economic life, the straight-line percentage of loss each year is calculated by dividing 100% of the replacement cost by the economic life.

> **For Example**
>
> Annual Depreciation = 100% of Cost ÷ Economic Life
>
> With an economic life of 10 years, the annual loss would be 100% ÷ 10 or 10%.
>
> With an economic life of 20 years, 100% ÷ 20 = 5% loss per year.
>
> With an economic life of 50 years, 100% ÷ 50 = 2% loss per year.

In order to estimate the depreciation, the appraiser estimates the property's age. Normally, the appraiser uses effective age after curing any curable depreciation, rather than actual age, in these calculations.

The appraiser then:
- multiplies the annual rate of depreciation by the effective age to determine the total percentage of value lost.
- multiplies that percentage by the replacement cost of the improvements (not by the current value of the building) to arrive at the dollar amount of the loss.

Total Depreciation = (Annual Depreciation x Effective Age) x Cost

The final step in the process is to deduct the depreciation of the improvements to arrive at the current market value of the property.

>   Land
>   + Cost of improvements
>   <u>- Depreciation</u>
>   Current property value

As a mathematical alternative, the appraiser could add the current value of the improvements to the value of the land. The current value of improvements is the percentage of their replacement cost after deducting depreciation. So, if total depreciation were 20%, the current value of the improvements would be 80% of the cost.

Real Estate Appraisal and Investments

Current Value = (100% - Depreciation) x Cost

> Land
> + Current value of improvements
> Current property value

Income Approach

The third appraisal approach is the **income approach** (or **capitalization approach**). This approach is used to appraise properties capable of producing rental income for the owner, i.e., apartments, office buildings, warehouses, etc. It bases the value of the property on the income the owner will receive and the rate of return the owner should find acceptable. The premise for this approach is that value is the present worth of future benefits: Value equals the price a person pays today for the right to receive net income from the property in the future.

The formula for this approach is $I = R \times V$. It can be remembered as IRV. **IRV** stands for income, rate and value:
- I (income) is the anticipated annual net income to be produced by the property.
- R (rate) is the capitalization rate.
- V (value) is the present worth of the property.

Since the net income is a percentage of the value, in estimating value, the income is divided by the rate: $I = R \times V$; therefore $I \div R = V$

> **For Example**
> The net income is $200,000 and the capitalization rate is 10%:
>   Value = $200,000 ÷ 10% = $2,000,000.
>
> The net income is $15,000 and the capitalization rate is 8%:
>   Value = $15,000 ÷ 8% = $187,500.

Net income is gross income less operating expenses. To estimate the net income, the appraiser must establish the property's gross income, or **scheduled gross income**. This is the total potential income from all sources, i.e., rental income, income from vending machines, parking, etc. It is not the current rent schedule but a figure of what the rents should be after an analysis of:
- historical rent (rent paid by the tenants in past years).
- contract rent (rent currently paid by the tenants).
- economic or market rent (the amount of rental income that could be obtained if the property were vacant and ready to be rented out, or were used at its highest and best use).

Once the scheduled gross income has been estimated, it is adjusted to account for the fact that there are likely to be vacancies and unpaid rents during the course of the year. Looking at past and present vacancy and collection loss rates for the property as well as the rates for comparable properties, the appraiser would determine a reasonable percentage of the scheduled gross rent anticipated to be lost. When vacancies and collection losses are deducted from scheduled gross income, the resulting figure is called effective gross income. **Effective gross income** equals scheduled gross income less vacancies and collection losses.

The next step is to estimate operating expenses. **Operating expenses** include fixed expenses, variable expenses and reserves for replacement:

- **Fixed expenses** are costs that are relatively permanent. They do not vary according to occupancy, e.g., real property taxes and property insurance.
- **Variable expenses** are costs that vary according to occupancy, such as fuel, utilities, decorating, repairs, advertising, and management. Management is the most easily overlooked item as it is not always accounted for by owners. A reasonable cost should be estimated even if the current owner has a particularly cost-effective way of handling management.
- **Reserves for replacement** are amounts set aside for replacing equipment or portions of the building that have a relatively short life expectancy. For example, if the ranges and refrigerators have an economic life of 10 years, the appraiser would estimate 1/10 of their replacement cost as an annual expense.

> **NOTE:** Deducted expenses do not include income tax payments, depreciation, or mortgage interest payments.

```
  Scheduled Gross
− Vacancies and Collection Losses
  Effective Gross
− Fixed Expenses
− Variable Expenses
− Reserves for Replacement
  Net Income
```

In addition to the quantity of income, the appraiser must consider the quality and durability of the income:

- Quality relates to the stability of the tenants and the likelihood that they will continue to pay rent.
- Durability relates to the period of time the income can be expected to continue; e.g., 5 years, 10 years, or 20 years.

Quality and durability of income are accounted for in the capitalization rate. The **capitalization rate** is a rate of return that converts net income to value. It relates the net income to the value, and it mathematically converts the net income figure to a value figure. If proper, it will attract investors with a number of investment options available to them to the property. The overall capitalization rate consists of a return *on* the investment and a return *of* the investment.

The overall capitalization rate includes an amount to provide the investor with a profit. It is called the return on the investment or the discount rate. It reflects a return to:
- equal a safe rate offered by government bonds or banks on savings accounts.
- compensate for risk (the greater the risk, the greater the amount to be added for risk).
- compensate for lack of liquidity (how long it may take to convert the real estate to cash).
- compensate for management of the investment (the time and effort involved in handling the investment itself).

Added to the return on the investment is a **recapture rate**. This is a rate of return of the investment in the improvement (or accrual for depreciation). If, due to depreciation of the building, there were a 2% annual loss of value to the property, the investor would need a 2% return for recapture of his investment in addition to the rate desired for the return on his investment.

Once a capitalization (cap) rate has been determined, the appraiser can capitalize the income, by dividing the net income by the capitalization rate, to get the value.

> **For Example**
>
> If net income is $40,000 and the capitalization rate is 10%, the value would be $40,000 ÷ 10%, or $400,000. (V = I÷R)
>
> If net income is $40,000 and the capitalization rate is 20%, the value would be $40,000 ÷ 20%, or $200,000.

> **NOTE:** The higher rate produces a lower value, since a higher rate implies a greater risk.

Gross Rent Multiplier

For smaller income properties, such as single-family homes or duplexes, in areas where the property might be purchased either for use as a residence or use as an income producer, a **gross rent multiplier** is used instead of the income approach. While it uses the same method as the sales comparison approach, the gross rent multiplier is considered the income approach for residential properties.

A gross rent multiplier is a factor. If this factor is multiplied by the rental price of a property, the result is an estimated market value. The formula for using a gross rent multiplier is as simple as remembering its name.

Value = Gross Rent x the Multiplier

An appraiser can arrive at a multiplier by dividing sales prices of comparable properties that have changed hands recently by the rents being charged at the time of the sale. An appropriate multiplier for the subject property can be calculated by adjusting to account for differences between the subject property and comparable properties.

Sales Price ÷ Gross Rent = Multiplier

After estimating the fair market rental for the subject property, based on comparable rental properties, the appraiser would multiply the estimated rent by the multiplier to get the estimated property value.

> **For Example**
>
> If rental properties in the area were selling for about 127 times their rents and the subject property was renting for $920 per month, its value would be 127 x $920, or $116,840.

	Subject Property	Rental #1	Rental #2	Rental #3
Location	1385 Main	1374 Main	1368 Main	1366 Main
Date of Sale		8/14	10/4	8/28
Price		$139,200	$121,600	$135,200
Date of Occupancy		6/1	7/1	8/1
Monthly Rent	$920	$1080	$960	$1080
Multiplier		139,200 ÷ 1080 = 129	121,600 ÷ 960 = 127	135,200 ÷ 1080 = 125

Indicated Multiplier: 127

Indicated Value: $920 x 127 = 116,840 (Rounded to $116,800)

> **NOTE:** The rental figures used are gross monthly rents. When appraising industrial or commercial properties or other properties that produce income other than from rents, an appraiser might use gross annual income. In these cases, the multiplier would be called a gross income multiplier, rather than a gross rent multiplier.

Reconciliation

All three appraisal methods (sales comparison, cost, and income) have at least something to contribute in the valuation of a property. So all are considered and used when practical. Each serves as a check against the others and narrows the range within which a final estimate of value falls. However, not all approaches are equally appropriate for a particular property. Therefore, the appraiser would never simply average the values obtained by the use of each of these approaches. Instead, he would interpret the data obtained and apply to each of his value estimates a weight proportionate to its merits in the particular instance. He would give the most weight to the income approach for income property, the sales comparison approach for marketable property, and the cost approach for property not commonly bought and sold in the market (such as churches and public buildings). This weighing, called **correlation or reconciliation**, is the final step in estimating the market value.

Real Estate Appraisal and Investments

Report

Once correlation is completed, the last step is reporting the value to the client. The report most commonly used is the summary report, or form report. This consists of one or more sheets, providing data about the neighborhood and property. An example of this is the Uniform Residential Appraisal Report, used by most lending institutions. A restricted report, or letter form report, is a signed, dated report providing only a description of the property, the type of value estimated, the purpose of the appraisal, and the value conclusion. A self-contained report, or narrative report, is the most complete type of appraisal report. It provides the value conclusion plus, the reasoning, computations, maps, photographs, charts and plats supporting the conclusion.

Appraisal Approaches

Approach (also called)	Best used for	Features
Cost Approach (Summation)	Unique or new buildings	• Separate land and building • Upper limit of value
Market Data (Sales Comparison)	Homes (amenities) and land	• Adjusts comparables
Income (Capitalization)	Rental Properties	• Capitalization – convert net income to value • Higher the risk, higher the rate, means a lower value

Real Estate Investments

People invest money with the idea of making a profit through income and/or growth in their capital. At the same time they may consider preserving their capital and minimizing their risks. The choices of investments include stocks, bonds, mutual funds, mortgage loans, certificates of deposit, commodities, and real estate.

Within the area of real estate there are numerous investment choices, such as houses, apartments, condominiums, raw land, farmland, vacant lots, retail stores, shopping centers, office buildings, mini warehouses, industrial properties, mobile home parks, and recreational developments. Some of these choices offer a return resulting from rental income, while others offer a return resulting from a gain upon sale of the property. Some others offer both.

Real estate investing is the purchase ownership, management and rental of real estate for a profit. Real estate investors need to be very careful since real estate in not nearly as easily traded or sold as other investments such as stocks or bonds. While many real estate investors may invest in single family homes or duplexes, etc., larger real estate investors invest in commercial or income properties.

The broad category of real estate investments is Income Property since investing in real estate is expected to produce a return or income from the property. Commercial real estate is a property that is owned to produce an income for the owner. It includes office buildings, strip malls, large shopping centers and hotels, as well as apartment buildings and even vacant land to be leased.

Industrial real estate is property that is used for manufacturing. An investor may build a building for a particular company so they can manufacture their product. The investor then leases the building to the manufacturer. This type of real estate is usually only usable by one manufacturer or type of manufacturing. For this reason, industrial leases are usually the longest of commercial leases since a vacancy would be difficult or even impossible to fill.

There are numerous advantages and disadvantages inherent in real estate investments.

----- INVESTMENT DISADVANTAGES AND ADVANTAGES -----

Disadvantages

Real estate has greater risks than many other investments.

A person must be more knowledgeable about the investment than if he is investing in mutual funds, bonds or certificates of deposit. He must be able to analyze neighborhood and economic trends, the structural improvements, the quality of potential tenants, tax consequences, and the most suitable financing terms.

Real estate lacks liquidity. Liquidity refers to the ease of converting the asset to cash. It is not always easy to convert a real estate asset to cash. Depending on the market, it may be difficult to refinance and take cash from the property, or it may take time to find a buyer and for the buyer to obtain a loan to provide needed cash.

Real estate is a long-term investment. It generally takes at least three to five years to make a reasonable profit on real estate.

Real estate also requires more management than other investments.

There is the risk of unfavorable legislation. Changes in tax codes, building codes, zoning ordinances, environmental controls, tenant-landlord laws, and rent controls may adversely affect the ownership of real estate as an investment.

Advantages

Real estate investment offers significant advantages. Because of the greater risks, real estate has historically produced a higher rate of return or yield (which relates the amount of money received to the amount invested) than other investments. This high rate of return may result from rental income, appreciation in value, and/or a gain in value due to sound management and planning.

Real estate is also a hedge against inflation. In times of inflation, as dollars lose their value, the worth of a bond or mortgage decreases as it will be repaid with dollars with less spending power. However, the value of real estate and other equity assets (i.e., ownership interests rather than creditor interests) increases as it will cost more of the cheapened dollars to buy the same property.

Another advantage to real estate is its use as collateral for a loan, allowing the owner to apply leverage. **Leverage** means using financing to allow a small amount of cash to purchase a large property investment. Real estate offers excellent leverage opportunities. To buy $200,000 worth of gold, it might cost $200,000 of the investor's money to make the purchase. To buy a $200,000 house, a person may be able to do so with anywhere from 0 to 20% down. Leverage provides the opportunity to make a large investment with only a little cash.

----- INVESTMENT PURPOSES -----

People may purchase real estate for a number of different purposes. Depending on the purpose for which the property is held, the Federal Tax Code will create different tax consequences, which may be significant to the owner.
Uses include:
- personal use, such as a personal residence (home). A personal residence may be a single-family home, a condominium or cooperative unit, a houseboat, or mobile home, or even one unit of a duplex, triplex or four-plex. The residence may be a principal residence, a second residence, or other property used to provide housing for family members. A principal residence is the owner's main home, the place where the owner lives most of the time. A second residence includes a residence used part time by the owner (e.g., a beach or mountain property).
- investment, with the expectation of profiting from an increase in value prior to resale, such as investing in unimproved land.
- production of income. This is property used to produce rental income for the owner (apartments, office buildings, etc.).
- use in the owner's principal trade or business. This may include a factory owned by the manufacturer, a company-owned office building, etc.
- sale to customers. This is property acquired by a developer, builder or investor in order to be resold for a profit in the ordinary course of business. It is also known as dealer property.

----- FEDERAL INCOME TAX -----

To understand the tax consequences of owning real property, it is necessary to understand some significant aspects of our Federal Tax Code.

Income Taxes
Income taxes are considered progressive taxes because the tax rates increase as taxable income increases. Persons earning higher incomes pay a higher percentage of their income than do persons earning less.

Taxable Income
Taxable income is the income on which tax is paid. Taxable income is gross income less certain tax deductions. Gross income includes all income, regardless of its source, unless the income is specifically excluded by the Internal Revenue Code (IRC).

Tax Deductions
Items which can be deducted from gross income to arrive at annual taxable income are called **tax deductions**.

For personal residences there is:
- a deduction for real property taxes.
- a deduction for mortgage interest (and loan origination fee, points and prepayment penalties) on up to $1,000,000 of debt for the acquisition, construction, or improvement of a primary and/or secondary home, or up to $100,000 total home equity debt on both homes.
- no deduction for depreciation, repairs or maintenance, or other operating expenses.

For investment property and property used in trade or business, there is:
- a deduction from annual income for operating expenses, repairs, maintenance and mortgage interest.
- a deduction for business expenses and expenses in producing rents, fees and commissions for services.
- a deduction for property taxes, property and liability insurance premiums, and uninsured casualty losses.
- a deduction for depreciation (cost recovery). The owner can assume the same amount of decrease in the value of his improvements each year. This is called straight line depreciation. The amount of depreciation that can be deducted annually is 100% of the amount paid for the asset divided by 27.5 years for residential property, or by 39 years for nonresidential property. This means for an apartment building, the annual depreciation deduction is about 3.6% of the cost of the improvements. For nonresidential property, the annual deduction is about 2.6%. The amount paid for the asset does not include the cost of the land, as land is never depreciated.

The depreciation deduction serves as a tax shelter by reducing taxable income without incurring any actual expense in the year of the deduction. However, when the property is sold, the taxpayer must pay tax of 25% on the total accumulated depreciation.

> **For Example**
> Barb Dwyer paid $100,000 for the improvements on a rental property. Each year, for 10 years, she claimed a tax deduction of $3,600 for depreciation. During those years, she was in the 30% tax bracket. Over the 10 years, she saved $10,800 (30% x $36,000) in taxes. When she sold her property, she had to pay back $9,000 in taxes on the claimed depreciation (25% x $36,000). The 25% rate she had to pay was less than the 30% she would have paid had she not taken the deduction.

> **NOTE:** If he does not claim the depreciation deduction to which he is entitled, the government will impute the deduction, and he will have to pay tax upon the sale of the asset as if he had taken the deduction.

Tax Credits

A **tax credit** is of greater value than an equal dollar amount of tax deductions. A tax credit is a direct deduction from the tax due, rather than a deduction from taxable income. For example, if a person is in the 30% tax bracket, a tax deduction of $1,000 will reduce that person's taxable income by $1,000 and reduce taxes by $300. If that same person had a $1,000 tax credit, his taxes owed would be reduced by $1,000.

Tax Aspects of Transferring Title to Real Property

People who sell property pay income tax on the net total of their capital gains and this includes the sale of real property. Capital gains are taxed at a preferential rate in comparison to ordinary income. The amount an investor is taxed depends on both his tax bracket, and the amount of time the investment was held before being sold. **Short-term capital gains** are taxed at the investor's ordinary income tax rate, and are investments held for a year or less before being sold. **Long-term capital gains** are gains on dispositions of assets held for more than a year, and are taxed at a lower rate than short-term gains.

In real estate, capital gains are based not on what is paid for the home, but on its **adjusted cost basis**. To calculate this:
- Take the purchase price of the home.
- Add adjustments:
    - Cost of the purchase, including inspections, transfer fees, attorney fees, inspections, but not points paid on the mortgage loan.
    - Cost of sale, including attorney's fees, real estate commissions, and money spent to fix up the home immediately prior to sale.
    - Cost of improvements, including additions, swimming pools, decks, etc. Improvements do not include repairing or replacing something already there, such as putting on a new roof or buying new hot water heater.
- The total is the adjusted cost basis of the home.
- Subtract the adjusted cost basis from the amount for which the home is sold. This is the capital gain.

Example:

Original Purchase Price:	$250,000
Plus	+
Improvements (New deck):	$ 50,000
Subtotal (Adjusted cost basis):	$300,000
Net Sales Price	$500,000
Minus:	-
Adjusted cost basis:	$300,000
Capital Gain:	$200,000

NOTE: This is a simple example that does not take into account such items as depreciation. Always refer a client to a tax professional for tax advice.

Capital Gains

When real property is sold, or disposed of, there are further tax consequences. For most types of real property, the profit realized upon disposition is considered a **capital gain**. In some instances, a loss realized upon disposition is considered a **capital loss**. Capital gains are gains on the disposition of assets. They are subject to taxation. Capital losses on the disposition of assets may be tax deductible. Capital gains are taxed at the normal tax rate, if the asset had been held for one year or less, and at a rate of up to 15%, if the assets had been held for more than one year.

A loss on the sale of real property is tax deductible, except for property held as a personal residence. Losses on income and investment property are capital losses. These losses are fully deductible from capital gains. If they exceed the capital gains, up to $3,000 of net capital losses may be deducted from ordinary income each year. Losses on dealer property and property used in a trade or business are ordinary losses.

In order to determine whether there is a gain or loss and the amount of the gain or loss, an owner must compare his adjusted basis in the property and the realized selling price of the property.

Determination of the adjusted basis starts with the original cost basis of the property. The **cost basis** is the purchase price of the property plus certain closing costs (such as legal fees and title insurance). This basis may be increased or decreased to arrive at the **adjusted basis**.

The basis is increased by the amount of assessments for local improvements (such as streets and sidewalks), and the amount paid for capital improvements, additions and other capital items. Capital improvements are items that add to the value of the property, prolong its useful life or adapt it to new uses.

The basis is reduced by the amount of uninsured losses from fire or other casualty, amounts previously deducted for depreciation, and payments received from the sale of any rights in or any part of the property.

Adjusted Cost Basis

```
  Original Basis
+ Assessments, Capital Improvements, Additions, etc.
- Depreciation Deductions, Uninsured Losses,
  Payments For Sale of Rights In or Part of the Property
  Adjusted Cost Basis
```

Determination of the **amount realized** from the sale of real property starts with the selling price. This is the total amount received for the property, including money, notes, mortgages and the value of any other property received. The amount realized is the selling price less selling expenses, such as commissions, advertising, legal fees, loan placement fees or discount points paid by the seller.

Amount Realized

```
  Selling Price
- Selling Expenses
  Amount Realized
```

The capital gain is then determined by subtracting the adjusted cost basis from the amount realized from the sale.

The fact that one makes a profit on the sale of real estate does not mean that tax must be paid on the gain that year. A gain is realized in the tax year in which the property is sold. The gain is recognized in the tax year for which it is taxed.

Capital Gain

Amount Realized
− Adjusted Cost Basis
Capital Gain (or Loss)

- Realized in the tax year in which property sold
- Recognized in the tax year for which it is taxed

Installment Sales

A person may defer tax on a gain (so it is recognized in a different year than it is realized) by use of an **installment sale**. If an owner sells real property in one year but does not receive full payment on the purchase price that year, it is an installment sale. The seller pays tax only on the amount of the capital gain he receives each year, based on the percentage the realized capital gain is to the contract sales price (e.g., if his gain were ¼ of the sales price, he would pay capital gains tax on ¼ of the principal payments received each year), plus tax on any interest received.

In the past, many sellers sold property on an installment sale at an artificially high price and artificially low interest rate, in order to be able to pay less tax on interest (which is taxed at ordinary tax rates) and more tax on the capital gain (which is taxed at lower tax rates). To stop this, the government imputes interest when a taxpayer loans money at an interest rate below the market rate and taxes the taxpayer as if he had received the interest he should have charged.

Primary Residence Exclusion from Capital Gains Tax

An individual may exclude, from his gross income up to $250,000 ($500,000 for a married couple filing jointly) of capital gains on the sale of real property if he used it as his primary residence for two of the five years before the date of sale. The two years of residency do not have to be continuous; the individual may meet the ownership and use tests during different two-year periods. However, both tests must be satisfied during the five-year period ending on the date of the sale. There are allowances and exceptions for military service, disability, partial residence and other reasons.

Tax-Deferred Exchanges

Taxes may also be deferred through use of a **taxed-deferred exchange (tax-free exchange, nontaxable exchange,** or **Section 1031 exchange)**. It is sometimes referred to as a 1031 exchange because Section 1031 of the Internal Revenue Code (IRC) establishes the requirements relating to such an exchange.

The most common type of tax-deferred exchange is a like-kind exchange. A **like-kind exchange** (or like-for-like exchange) is an exchange of tangible like-kind properties, (e.g., real estate for real estate or personal property for personal property, but not real property for personal property). The exchange must involve only business, income or investment property. Neither property in the exchange may be used by the taxpayer for personal purposes, such as a home, or be dealer property, held for sale to customers. Within these guidelines virtually any type of properties could be exchanged. Therefore, a store building used in business could be exchanged for an apartment house used as an investment, since both are real property and neither is used for personal use or as dealer property.

The exchange of properties may be simultaneous or may be delayed. A **delayed exchange** actually involves a sale with the sale proceeds held by a facilitator. These funds are then used to make a purchase of property to replace the property sold. To qualify for the tax deferral in a delayed exchange, the taxpayer must identify potential replacement property within 45 days and actually take title to property identified within 180 days after the date he transfers title to the property given up in the exchange.

If the transaction qualifies as a tax-deferred exchange, the taxpayer will pay tax only on the lesser of his gain or boot received. **Boot** is money, unlike property or an assumption of a greater mortgage balance (mortgage relief) the taxpayer has received in the exchange. It arises from the difference between his equity in the property he gave up and his equity in the property received. If he pays boot, his entire gain would be deferred. If he receives boot, he would pay tax on the lesser of his gain or the boot received.

> **For Example**
>
> Ann and Bob exchange real property. Ann has property worth $140,000, with a $30,000 loan balance outstanding. Bob has real property worth $100,000 which is owned free and clear. Ann's equity (i.e., the difference between the property value and the liens encumbering the property) is $110,000; Bob's is $100,000. Therefore, Bob will give Ann $10,000 cash to balance their equities. Ann is receiving $40,000 of boot, consisting of $10,000 cash and $30,000 mortgage relief. In exchange, each party pays tax on their realized gain or boot received, whichever is less (so Ann must pay tax on $40,000 or her gain, whichever is less, and Bob can defer all of his gain and pay no tax, since he received no boot).

Ann	Bob
$140,000 Real Estate	$100,000 Real Estate
- $30,000 Loan Balance	
$110,000 Equity	$100,000 Equity
	+ $ 10,000 Cash

	$110,000
Receives $40,000 boot	Receives No boot

Gains can continue to be deferred as a result of additional exchanges, as a person trades up into greater equity (the difference between the property value and the liens encumbering the property). The total gain is partially taxed as one trades down, receiving boot for some of the equity, or fully taxed when one sells the property, receiving boot for the entire equity.

Tax Exemptions

A homeowner is eligible for a major tax break on the sale of a home. If he has owned and lived in a home as his main home two of the past five years and has not excluded any gain on the sale of another home in the past two years, he may exempt $250,000 of gain. Therefore, if a person sells his home of two years and realizes a gain of $200,000, none of the gain is taxable. If he realizes a gain of $300,000, only $50,000 is taxable at the capital gains rate.

If there are co-owners, each is entitled to a separate exemption, if qualified. When a married couple files a joint return and each spouse has lived in the home as a main home two of the past five years and has not excluded any gain on the sale of another home in the past two years, the exemption is $500,000 of gain, even if only one spouse has owned the property for the required two years.

The exemption is prorated if the two-year requirement is not met due to health, employment or special circumstances.

Brain Teaser

Reinforce your understanding of the material by correctly completing the following sentences:

1. The three basic physical characteristics of real estate are _____, _____ and _____.

2. _____ results when improvements begin to lose acceptability to prospective purchasers or renters.

3. Because it uses comparison, the sales comparison approach is based on the theory of _____.

4. The income (_____) approach is used to appraise properties capable of producing rental income for the owners.

5. A loss on the sale of real property is not deductible for property held as a _____ residence.

Brain Teaser Answers

1. The three basic physical characteristics of real estate are **immobility**, **indestructibility** and **heterogeneity**.

2. **Depreciation** results when improvements begin to lose acceptability to prospective purchasers or renters.

3. Because it uses comparison, the sales comparison approach is based on the theory of **substitution**.

4. The income (**capitalization**) approach is used to appraise properties capable of producing rental income for the owner.

5. A loss on the sale of real property is not deductible for property held as a **personal** residence.

Review — Real Estate Appraisal and Investments

In this lesson we discuss real property appraisal and elements of real estate investment.

Valuation and Appraisal

Value is the relationship between items and persons wanting those items. Differences in value are caused by four characteristics of value: the item's utility, scarcity, and transferability and demand. The value of real estate is influenced by its physical characteristics: its immobility, indestructibility and inhomogeneity or heterogeneity, and by four general forces: physical and environmental characteristics, economic conditions, governmental regulations and social influences.

Market value is the "most probable price which a property should bring in a competitive and open market under all conditions requisite to a fair sale, the buyer and seller each acting prudently and knowledgably, and assuming the price is not affected by undue stimulus," and is determined by buyers and sellers. Appraisers give an informed opinion when estimating the value of property. The most complete appraisal report is a narrative report. The appraiser uses different approaches, then analyzes and compares the results of each in a process called reconciliation or correlation.

The characteristics of real property lead to certain economic concepts and principles relating to the valuation of real property. The principle of highest and best use holds that the maximum value of land exists when the property is used for its highest and best use. This is the possible, feasible, and legally permissible use that, at the time of the appraisal, is most likely to yield the greatest net return over a given period of time.

Principle of Substitution

The principle of substitution holds that, if a property is replaceable, its value tends to be set by the cost of acquiring, by purchase or construction, an equally desirable substitute property without any undue delay. This principle is the basis for all of the approaches used to estimate value: the sales comparison (or market data) approach, the income (or capitalization) approach, and the cost approach.

- The market data approach is the main valuation principle and holds that a prudent person would not pay more for a product than he would pay for a reasonable substitute.
- The income approach holds that a person would not accept a lower rate of return than from a reasonable substitute.
- The cost approach holds that a person would not pay more than it would cost to build a reasonable substitute.

Sales Comparison Approach

The sales comparison approach is a valuation of properties by comparing prices paid for similar properties. It is most likely to be used in appraising residential properties and land. In this approach, the appraiser collects and verifies sales data and compares the subject property to comparable properties in terms of location, time of sale, terms and conditions of sale, and physical characteristics (including amenities). Amenities are features that add to a property's desirability. Conditions of sale should not include foreclosures or other types of sales not in an open market. Where the properties differ, adjustments are made to the sales price of the comparable property (down if the subject property is not as good as the comparable, or up if it is better) to bring it to the price for which the subject property should sell.

Income (Capitalization) Approach

The income (capitalization) approach is used to appraise properties that produce income by evaluating their net income and converting it to a value estimate. For income property, the value would be the present worth of future potential benefits, i.e., the anticipated net income to be obtained from the property. The estimated net income is calculated by subtracting an allowance for vacancies and bad debts from the scheduled gross income to arrive at an effective gross income, and then subtracting operating expenses (maintenance, repairs, management, etc.), fixed expenses (taxes and insurance), and reserves for replacement of items that wear out.

The greater the risk of the investment, the higher the capitalization rate the investor wants; the higher the rate, the lower the value of the property.

To calculate the value, the appraiser divides the estimated annual net income of the property by a capitalization rate. The capitalization rate is the rate of return the new owner can expect to receive, including a rate of return of the investment necessary to recapture depreciation costs. In calculating straight-line depreciation, an appraiser assumes that 100% of the property's cost will be lost by the end of its economic life (the period of time in which a building produces sufficient income to justify its continued use). Therefore, the annual recapture rate is determined by dividing 100% of the replacement cost by the economic life of the improvement.

For houses used as rental properties, a gross rent multiplier might be used. The value of a rental property is estimated by multiplying its estimated monthly rent by an appropriate multiplier. The multiplier is derived by dividing the sales prices of comparable houses that have sold by their monthly rents.

Cost Approach

While the cost approach can be used for any property, it is most often used to appraise value in use for new buildings, where costs are easy to obtain, and for properties such as churches and public service buildings that cannot be compared to others that have sold or to those that produce income. The appraiser estimates the value of the land and the depreciated value of the improvements on the land separately and adds the two values to arrive at an estimate of the property's total value.

The most commonly used method to estimate the cost of residential property is the square foot method, using the average cost per square foot of living area to construct a building of the same type and quality. The total value of the land and the cost new of improvements, before deducting depreciation, is the upper limit of the value of the property.

Depreciation

Depreciation is a loss in value due to any cause. Causes include physical deterioration, functional obsolescence, and economic obsolescence. Physical deterioration is reflected in items in need of repair or replacement due to natural causes (like dry rot or termite damage), wear and tear, and deferred maintenance. An appraiser places the greatest emphasis on the observed condition of the building in calculating this depreciation. Rather than estimate depreciation based on the building's actual age, he estimates the building's effective age, i.e., its age based on its condition. A building has a lower effective age if well maintained, and a higher effective age if poorly maintained:

- Depreciated value equals the cost to replace or reproduce the improvements less depreciation.
- Replacement cost is the present cost of constructing a new substitute structure, equal to the existing structure in quality and utility, but using current construction methods, materials, design and layout.
- Reproduction cost is the present cost of constructing a new substitute structure that is an exact replica of the existing structure.

Functional obsolescence results from loss of functionality due to basic construction techniques used, as well as inadequacy (e.g., a single-car garage, a small water heater), outdatedness, or overadequacy in a building. Economic obsolescence results from factors outside and surrounding the property, such as zoning, blight, high taxes, and pollution, and is, therefore, almost always incurable.

Real estate and other equity assets are hedges against inflation, as their value should increase as the value of the dollar decreases. Equity is the difference between the property value and the liens encumbering the property.

Tax Implications

Real estate owners are able to take tax deductions for personal residences and second homes. The owner may deduct real property taxes and mortgage interest, but he may not deduct depreciation, repairs or maintenance, or other operating expenses. For investment property and property used in a trade or business, the owner may deduct operating expenses, repairs, maintenance, and mortgage interest from annual income. They may also deduct business expenses, fees and commissions for services, property taxes, property and liability insurance premiums, and depreciation.

The profit realized upon disposition of real estate is considered a capital gain. It is determined by subtracting the adjusted cost basis from the amount realized from the sale. Capital gains are taxed at a rate of up to 15%, if the assets have been held for more than one year. However, a homeowner occupying a house as his main home two of the past five years can exempt $250,000 of gain ($500,000 if filing a joint return). A property owner may defer tax on a gain by use of an installment sale or a tax-deferred (1031) exchange involving like-kind business or investment real property. In an exchange, each party pays taxes on his realized gain or unlike property received, whichever is less. Unlike property received in an exchange of real property, such as cash, is called boot.

Accruals for depreciation 84
Accrued depreciation 84
Actual age 85
Adjustable-rate mortgage (ARM) . 50, 12
Adjusted basis 102
Adjusted cost basis 101
Age-life method 91
Agreement of sale 10
Alienation clause 4
Amenities 82
Amortized loan.................................... 13
Amount realized 102
Annual percentage rate (APR) 21
Anticipation... 80
Appraisal 83
Assemblage 82
Assignment of rents clause 7
Assume and agree to pay 5
Balloon payment 13
Beneficiary 9
Blanket mortgage 16
Blind assumption 42
Boot 104
Budget mortgage 14
Capital gain 101
Capital loss 101
Capitalization approach 92
Capitalization rate 93
Certificate of eligibility 42
Certificate of reasonable value (CRV) 43
Change 80
Chattel mortgage 15
Closed-end mortgage 17
CMA 74
Commercial banks 34
Comparative cost method 90
Compensating factors 46
Competition.. 81
Competitive market analysis 74
Compound interest 48
Conforming loans............................... 37
Conformity 80
Construction mortgage 17
Consumer Credit Protection Act 20
Contract for deed............................... 10
Contribution 81

Conventional loans 39
Correlation 95
Cost 76
Cost approach 80, 89
Cost basis 102
Credit unions 34
Deed in lieu of foreclosure 15
Deed of trust 8
Defeasance clause 7
Deficiency judgment 8
Deflation 47
Delayed exchange 104
Depreciation 84

Direct principal reduction 14
Discount points 35
Discount rate 47
Economic life 86
Economic obsolescence 85
Effective age 85
Effective demand 77
Effective gross income 93
Effective interest rate 50
Endorsement 3
Equal Credit Opportunity Act (ECOA)
 23
Equitable right of redemption 8
Equitable title 10
External obsolescence 85
Fannie Mae 37
Farm Credit Bank 35
Federal Department of Veterans Affairs
(VA) 42
Federal Housing Administration (FHA)
 41
Federal Reserve System (the Fed) 47
FHA loan 40
FICO score 45
Finance charge 21
Finance companies 34
Financial Institutions Reform, Recovery,
and Enforcement Act (FIRREA) 74
First mortgage 14
Fiscal policy 47
Fixed expenses 93
Fixed-rate 50
Fixed-rate mortgage 12

Flexible-rate mortgage 12
Flood Disaster Protection Act 23
Foreclosure.. 61
Foreclosure sale 8
Freddie Mac 38
Fully amortized mortgage 13
Functional obsolescence 85
General forces 77
Ginnie Mae.. 38
Graduated payment mortgage 13
Grantor 9
Gross rent multiplier 94
HELOC 18
Home equity line of credit 18
Home equity loan 18
Income approach 80, 92
Income taxes 99
Increasing and diminishing returns 81
Inflation 47
Installment sale 103
Interest-only mortgage 12
Intermediate theory 6
Judicial foreclosure and sale 8
Jumbo loans 37
Junior mortgage 15
Land sales contract 10
Late payment penalty 4
Level payment mortgage...................... 13
Leverage 98
Lien theory 6
Life ipnsurance companies 34
Like-kind exchange 104
Loan-to-value ratio 39
Lock-in clause 4
Long-term capital gains 101
Market data approach 86
Market value 76
Monetary policy 47
Mortgage 6
Mortgage banker 33
Mortgage broker 32
Mortgagee 7
Mortgagor 7
Mutual mortgage insurance 42
Negative amortization 12
Negotiable instrument 3

Net income 92
Nominal interest rate 50

Non taxable exchange 103
Nonrecourse loan 8
Objective value 75
Obligatory advances 17
Obsolescence.. 85
Office of Federal Housing Enterprise Oversight (OFHEO) 44
Open market operations 48
Open-end mortgage 17
Operating expenses 93
Package mortgage 16
Partial reconveyance 16
Partial satisfaction 16
Partially amortized mortgage 13
Participation certificates 37
Participation mortgage 16
Pension funds 34
Physical deterioration 84
Physical life 86
PITI mortgage 14
Plottage 82
Power of sale clause 8
Predatory lending 45
Prepayment penalty 4
Prepayment privilege 4
Price 76
Primary mortgage market 32
Private individuals 35
Progression 81
Promissory note 3
Purchase money mortgage 10
Qualifying ratios 45
Quantity survey method 90
Real estate investment trust (REIT) 35
Real Estate Settlement Procedures Act (RESPA) 22
Recapture rate 94
Reconciliation 95
Regression 81
Regulation Z.. 20
Release clause 16
Renegotiated-rate mortgage 12
Replacement cost 89
Replacement cost approach 89

Reproduction cost 89
Reproduction cost approach 89
Request for notice of default 7
Reserve requirements 47
Reserves for replacement 93
Reverse annuity mortgage.................... 13
Reverse mortgage 13
Rollover mortgage 12
Rural housing service (RHS) 43
Sales comparison approach 80, 86
Satisfaction... 7
Savings banks....................................... 34
Scarcity 76
Scheduled gross income 92
Secondary mortgage market 36
Section 1031 exchange 103
Security agreement 15
Self-liquidating mortgage 13
Shared appreciation mortgage 17
Shared equity mortgage 17
Short-term capital gains 101
Simple interest 48
State certified general appraiser 74
State certified residential appraiser 74
State licensed appraiser 74
Statutory right of redemption 8
Straight mortgage 12

Straight-line method............................. 91
Strict foreclosure 8
Subjective value 75
Subordination clause 14
Subprime loans.................................... 44
Substitution 80
Summation approach 89
Supply and demand 81
Take out loan....................................... 18
Tax credit 100
Tax deductions 99
Taxable income 99
Taxed-deferred exchange 103
Tax-free exchange 103
Term mortgage 12
Title subject to..................................... 5
Title theory 6
Total of payments 21
Transferability 77

Term	Page
Trigger terms	22
Trust deed	8
Trustee	9
Trustor	9
Truth In Lending Act	20
Uniform residential appraisal report (URAR)	83
Unit in place method	90
Usury laws	46
Utility	76
VA loan	41
Valuation	74
Value	75
Variable expenses	93
Variable interest rates	50
Variable-rate mortgage	12
Vendee	10
Vendor	10
Warehousing	33, 36
Wraparound mortgage	15

9160

9860
104641
~~10580~~
~~1120~~ 9410